HowExpert Guide to Microbiology

101 Tips to Learn about the History, Applications, Research, Universities, and Careers in Microbiology

HowExpert with Sehrish Siddique

Copyright HowExpert™
www.HowExpert.com

For more tips related to this topic, visit HowExpert.com/microbiology

Recommended Resources

- HowExpert.com – Quick 'How To' Guides on All Topics from A to Z by Everyday Experts.
- HowExpert.com/free – Free HowExpert Email Newsletter.
- HowExpert.com/books – HowExpert Books
- HowExpert.com/courses – HowExpert Courses
- HowExpert.com/clothing – HowExpert Clothing
- HowExpert.com/membership – HowExpert Membership Site
- HowExpert.com/affiliates – HowExpert Affiliate Program
- HowExpert.com/jobs – HowExpert Jobs
- HowExpert.com/writers – Write About Your #1 Passion/Knowledge/Expertise & Become a HowExpert Author.
- HowExpert.com/resources – Additional HowExpert Recommended Resources
- YouTube.com/HowExpert – Subscribe to HowExpert YouTube.
- Instagram.com/HowExpert – Follow HowExpert on Instagram.
- Facebook.com/HowExpert – Follow HowExpert on Facebook.
- TikTok.com/@HowExpert – Follow HowExpert on TikTok.

Publisher's Foreword

Dear HowExpert Reader,

HowExpert publishes quick 'how to' guides on all topics from A to Z by everyday experts.

At HowExpert, our mission is to discover, empower, and maximize everyday people's talents to ultimately make a positive impact in the world for all topics from A to Z...one everyday expert at a time!

All of our HowExpert guides are written by everyday people just like you and me, who have a passion, knowledge, and expertise for a specific topic.

We take great pride in selecting everyday experts who have a passion, real-life experience in a topic, and excellent writing skills to teach you about the topic you are also passionate about and eager to learn.

We hope you get a lot of value from our HowExpert guides, and it can make a positive impact on your life in some way. All of our readers, including you, help us continue living our mission of positively impacting the world for all spheres of influences from A to Z.

If you enjoyed one of our HowExpert guides, then please take a moment to send us your feedback from wherever you got this book.

Thank you, and we wish you all the best in all aspects of life.

Sincerely,

BJ Min
Founder & Publisher of HowExpert
HowExpert.com

PS...If you are also interested in becoming a HowExpert author, then please visit our website at HowExpert.com/writers. Thank you & again, all the best!

COPYRIGHT, LEGAL NOTICE AND DISCLAIMER:

COPYRIGHT © BY HOWEXPERT™ (OWNED BY HOT METHODS). ALL RIGHTS RESERVED WORLDWIDE. NO PART OF THIS PUBLICATION MAY BE REPRODUCED IN ANY FORM OR BY ANY MEANS, INCLUDING SCANNING, PHOTOCOPYING, OR OTHERWISE WITHOUT PRIOR WRITTEN PERMISSION OF THE COPYRIGHT HOLDER.

DISCLAIMER AND TERMS OF USE: PLEASE NOTE THAT MUCH OF THIS PUBLICATION IS BASED ON PERSONAL EXPERIENCE AND ANECDOTAL EVIDENCE. ALTHOUGH THE AUTHOR AND PUBLISHER HAVE MADE EVERY REASONABLE ATTEMPT TO ACHIEVE COMPLETE ACCURACY OF THE CONTENT IN THIS GUIDE, THEY ASSUME NO RESPONSIBILITY FOR ERRORS OR OMISSIONS. ALSO, YOU SHOULD USE THIS INFORMATION AS YOU SEE FIT, AND AT YOUR OWN RISK. YOUR PARTICULAR SITUATION MAY NOT BE EXACTLY SUITED TO THE EXAMPLES ILLUSTRATED HERE; IN FACT, IT'S LIKELY THAT THEY WON'T BE THE SAME, AND YOU SHOULD ADJUST YOUR USE OF THE INFORMATION AND RECOMMENDATIONS ACCORDINGLY.

THE AUTHOR AND PUBLISHER DO NOT WARRANT THE PERFORMANCE, EFFECTIVENESS OR APPLICABILITY OF ANY SITES LISTED OR LINKED TO IN THIS BOOK. ALL LINKS ARE FOR INFORMATION PURPOSES ONLY AND ARE NOT WARRANTED FOR CONTENT, ACCURACY OR ANY OTHER IMPLIED OR EXPLICIT PURPOSE.

ANY TRADEMARKS, SERVICE MARKS, PRODUCT NAMES OR NAMED FEATURES ARE ASSUMED TO BE THE PROPERTY OF THEIR RESPECTIVE OWNERS, AND ARE USED ONLY FOR REFERENCE. THERE IS NO IMPLIED ENDORSEMENT IF WE USE ONE OF THESE TERMS.

NO PART OF THIS BOOK MAY BE REPRODUCED, STORED IN A RETRIEVAL SYSTEM, OR TRANSMITTED BY ANY OTHER MEANS: ELECTRONIC, MECHANICAL, PHOTOCOPYING, RECORDING, OR OTHERWISE, WITHOUT THE PRIOR WRITTEN PERMISSION OF THE AUTHOR.

ANY VIOLATION BY STEALING THIS BOOK OR DOWNLOADING OR SHARING IT ILLEGALLY WILL BE PROSECUTED BY LAWYERS TO THE FULLEST EXTENT. THIS PUBLICATION IS PROTECTED UNDER THE US COPYRIGHT ACT OF 1976 AND ALL OTHER APPLICABLE INTERNATIONAL, FEDERAL, STATE AND LOCAL LAWS AND ALL RIGHTS ARE RESERVED, INCLUDING RESALE RIGHTS: YOU ARE NOT ALLOWED TO GIVE OR SELL THIS GUIDE TO ANYONE ELSE.

THIS PUBLICATION IS DESIGNED TO PROVIDE ACCURATE AND AUTHORITATIVE INFORMATION WITH REGARD TO THE SUBJECT MATTER COVERED. IT IS SOLD WITH THE UNDERSTANDING THAT THE AUTHORS AND PUBLISHERS ARE NOT ENGAGED IN RENDERING LEGAL, FINANCIAL, OR OTHER PROFESSIONAL ADVICE. LAWS AND PRACTICES OFTEN VARY FROM STATE TO STATE AND IF LEGAL OR OTHER EXPERT ASSISTANCE IS REQUIRED, THE SERVICES OF A PROFESSIONAL SHOULD BE SOUGHT. THE AUTHORS AND PUBLISHER SPECIFICALLY DISCLAIM ANY LIABILITY THAT IS INCURRED FROM THE USE OR APPLICATION OF THE CONTENTS OF THIS BOOK.

COPYRIGHT BY HOWEXPERT™ (OWNED BY HOT METHODS)
ALL RIGHTS RESERVED WORLDWIDE.

Table of Contents

Recommended Resources 2

Publisher's Foreword 3

Chapter 1: Introduction to Microbiology 6

Chapter 2: History 30

Chapter 3: Applications of Microbiology 61

Chapter 4: Research 75

Chapter 5: Scope and Future Perspectives of Microbiology ... 139

FAQs 146

About the Expert 148

Recommended Resources 149

Chapter 1: Introduction to Microbiology

Tip 1: Get to know Microbiology

Welcome to the magnificent world of microbiology! So. Curious to know microbiology? If we break down the word "microbiology" in half, it will split into micro and biology. Micro means small, precisely up to 10^6 in size, and biology means the study of life. So microbiology refers to the study of microorganisms or microbes. Microbiology is a vast field that includes bacteriology, immunology, virology, parasitology mycology, and other branches. A person who is a specialist in microbiology and its related topics is known as a microbiologist. Microbiology is a quite young science, and there is a lot still to discover and understand. It's been three hundred years since we discovered the first bacteria, and still, many studies suggest that we have information about 1% of the microbes, 99% still be to be discovered. So in the eyes of the world, microbiology is still in its infancy.

Tip 2: Who are the Microbes?

 Microbes are an absolute requirement as they serve in all important aspects of human life, including the food we eat and the air we breathe. They are the potential agents of many human diseases. Microorganisms are diverse; they consist of algae, bacteria, protozoa, fungi, animals (such as planarians and rotifers), and green algae (microscopic plants). Some microbiologists also count viruses in the same category, while others view them as nonliving. Microorganisms are further classified as unicellular and multicellular. Most of the microbes are unicellular, but there are some multicellular microbes as well.

They are found everywhere in the biosphere where there is water, i.e., soil, ocean floor, atmosphere, hot springs, and Earth's crust. Microorganisms may be found in any section of the biosphere where there is liquid water, such as soil, the ocean floor, hot springs, deep inside rocks, high in the atmosphere, and the Earth's crust. Most significantly, these creatures are essential to people and the environment because they engage in Earth's element cycles, such as the nitrogen and carbon cycles. Microorganisms also play important functions in almost all ecosystems, such as waste products of other organisms through decomposition and recycling the dead remains. In addition, microbes play a crucial role as symbionts in most higher-order multicellular animals. They are also used in biotechnology, traditional food and beverage preparation, and current genetically engineered technologies. On the other hand, pathogenic microorganisms are hazardous because they infiltrate and thrive within other species, creating illnesses that kill humans, animals, and plants.

Tip 3: The Pathogenic Ecology of Microbes

Many microbes are helpful, while others cause infectious illnesses. Pathogenic bacteria, which often cause illnesses such as plague, TB, and anthrax, are among the species involved. Biofilms, which are microbial communities that are extremely difficult to eliminate, are estimated to be associated with illnesses such as bacterial infections in patients with cystic fibrosis, Legionnaires' disease, and otitis media. They form plaque and tartar, colonize catheters, transcutaneous, prostheses, and orthopedic devices, and contaminate contact lenses, broken skin, and burnt tissue.

Biofilms cause foodborne infections by colonizing the surfaces of food and food-processing devices. Biofilms pose a significant concern since they are resistant to the majority of bacterial growth control strategies. Furthermore, the overuse and misuse of antibiotics have resulted in a serious worldwide problem due to the selection of resistant strains of bacteria throughout time. A particularly hazardous strain, methicillin-resistant Staphylococcus aureus (MRSA), has recently wrought havoc.

Furthermore, protozoans have been linked to illnesses such as malaria, latent infection, and toxoplasmosis, while fungi have been linked to ringworm, candidiasis, and histoplasmosis. Viruses cause other illnesses such as influenza, yellow fever, and AIDS.

Food-related illnesses are caused by consuming contaminated food and pathogenic bacteria, viruses, or parasites that infect food. "Hygiene" is the prevention of infection or food spoilage by removing germs from the environment. Because microorganisms (bacteria in particular) are ubiquitous, the number of hazardous germs can be decreased to safety limits using adequate hygienic conditions. However, an object or substance must be fully sterilized in other situations. A sterile syringe is a perfect demonstration of this.

Tip 4: How do Microbes Interact with one Another?

Types and interactions of microbes are mutualism, competition, commensalism, proto-cooperation, predation, syntrophism, parasitism, and antagonism.

Interactions between microbes

Microorganisms engage with each other and can be physically linked to other organisms in a number of ways. For example, one species can exist as an ectobiont on the surface of another organism or as an endobiont within another organism. Microbial contact can be beneficial, such as mutualism, proto-cooperation, and commensalism, or it can be harmful, such as parasitism, predation, or competition.

Tip 5: Types of Microbial Interaction

Positive interaction	Negative interaction
Mutualism	Ammensalism (antagonism)
Proto-cooperation	Parasitism
Commensalism	Predation
	Competition

Tip 6: Mutualism

Mutualism is defined as a relationship in which each organism in an interaction benefit from the other's presence. It is a mutualistic interaction in which mutualist and host are metabolically reliant on one another. A mutualistic connection is one in which one of the members of the association cannot be replaced by another species. Mutualism necessitates intimate physical touch between organisms that interact. Mutualism permits organisms to survive in habitats that would be inaccessible to either species alone. Mutualistic relationships between organisms allow them to function as if they were one.

Example:

Lichens:

Lichens are a fantastic illustration of mutualism. They are a grouping of distinct fungus and a species of algae. In lichen, the fungal partner is referred to as a mycobiont, while the algal partner is referred to as an algobiont. A phycobiont is a member of the cyanobacteria and green algae families (Trabauxua). Because phycobionts are photoautotrophs, the fungus obtains its organic carbon directly from the algal partner; in exchange, the fungus shelters the phycobiont from harsh circumstances while also providing water and minerals to the algae. Lichens develop slowly but can form colonies in habitats that do not allow other species to flourish. Most lichens are resistant to heat and dryness.

Protozoan-termite interaction:

The protozoan-termite relationship is a famous example of mutualism in which flagellated protozoans reside in the guts of termites. These flagellated protozoans eat carbohydrates obtained as cellulose or lignin by their host termites and convert them into acetic acid, which termites use.

Chlorella-Paramecium:

Paramecium (ciliates) may host Chlorella (algae) in its cytoplasm. The algae Chlorella supply the protozoan partner with carbon and oxygen, while the protozoa in exchange give protection, motility, CO_2, and other growth factors. As long as there is enough light, the presence of Chlorella within Paramecium aids protozoa survival under anaerobic conditions.

Tip 7: Syntrophism

Syntrophism is a connection in which one organism's development is dependent on or enhanced by the substrate given by another organism. Both organisms in a connection benefit from syntrophism.

Example:

Non-pathogenic E. coli in human intestinal tract:

E. coli is a facultative anaerobe that utilizes oxygen and lowers the O_2 content in the gut, creating an environment ideal for obligate anaerobes such as Bacteroides. Bacteroides have no effect on E. coli as a host.

Flavobacterium (host) and Legionella pneumophila (commensal):

Flavobacterium excretes cystine, which Legionella pneumophila uses to live in aquatic environments. Nitrosomonas (host) and Nitrobacter (commensal) Cooperation in Nitrification: Nitrosomonas oxidizes ammonia to nitrite, which Nitrobacter then utilizes to acquire energy and oxidizes to nitrate.

Tip 8: Ammensalism (antagonism)

Flavobacterium excretes cystine, which Legionella pneumophila uses to live in aquatic environments. Nitrosomonas (host) and Nitrobacter (commensal) Cooperation in Nitrification: Nitrosomonas oxidizes ammonia to nitrite, which Nitrobacter then utilizes to acquire energy and oxidizes to nitrate.

Example:

Lactic acid generated by lactic acid bacteria: Lactic acid released by several normal floras in the vaginal tract inhibits the growth of many pathogenic species, including Candida albicans.

Skin normal flora: The fatty acid generated by skin flora prevents the growth of many harmful bacteria in the skin.

Thiobacillus thiooxidant: Thiobacillus thiooxidant releases sulfuric acid by sulfur oxidation, which causes a decrease in pH in the culture media, inhibiting the development of most other bacteria.

Tip 9: Competition

The competition shows a poor interaction between two microbial populations in which both populations suffer in terms of survival and growth. Competition occurs when two populations consume the same resources, such as the same space or nourishment, resulting in a decreased maximum density or growth rate for the microbial community. Microbial populations struggle for growth-limiting nutrients such as carbon, nitrogen, phosphorus, vitamins, growth hormones, and so on. Competition prevents both populations from inhabiting the same biological niche since one will win, and the other will be destroyed.

Example:

Competition between Paramecium caudatum and Paramecium aurelia: When these protozoa are brought together, both species of Paramecium feed on the same bacterium population. Due to competition, P. aurelia grows faster than P. caudatum.

Tip 10: Parasitism

It is a connection in which one population (parasite) benefits and obtains nutrients from another community (host) in the association that is hurt. The host-parasite interaction is distinguished by a relatively extended period of physical or metabolic contact. Some parasites reside outside the host cell and are known as ectoparasites, while others dwell inside the host cell and are known as endoparasites.

Viruses: They are obligatory intracellular parasites with high host specificity. There are several viruses that are parasites of bacteria (bacteriophage), fungus, algae, protozoa, and other organisms.

Bdellovibrio: Bdellovibrio is an ectoparasite of several gram-negative bacteria.

The parasite Bdellovibrio reaches the periplasmic space but not the host cytoplasm after penetrating the host's outer membrane.

Tip 11: Predation

Predation is a common event in which one creature (the predator) engulfs or attacks another organism (prey). Prey might be larger or smaller than the predator, which usually ends in the prey's death. Normally, predator-prey interactions are brief.

Example:

Protozoan-bacteria in soil: Protozoan bacteria in soil: Many protozoans can feast on diverse bacterial populations, which serve to maintain the number of soil bacteria at an optimal level.

Bdellovibrio, Vampirococcus, Daptobacter, and other predator bacteria can feed on a wide spectrum of bacteria population densities.

Tip 12: Microbial Evolution

Microbial evolution refers to genetically driven changes in microorganisms that persist over time. In addition, some microbial alterations may occur as a result of selection pressure. The many changes that may occur in bacteria in response to the presence of antibiotics are the greatest illustrations of this. These modifications can render bacteria less sensitive or entirely resistant to the killing activity of one or more antibiotics.

In the absence of any selection pressure, other microbial alterations can arise randomly. These alterations, which are frequently caused by a change in the sequence of the units (nucleotides) that form an organism's genetic material, might provide an advantage to the organism over unmodified species. In the traditional evolutionary scenario, such a favorable characteristic will be kept and passed on to future generations of the organism.

Even amongst species unrelated to one another, gene transfer can occur. This so-called horizontal gene transfer is a natural kind of microbial evolution that can be essential in infectious illness, such as acquiring a gene that determines antibiotic resistance.

Contrary to Darwinian evolution, which takes millions of years, microbial evolution may happen in hours. This is because, under perfect growth circumstances, certain bacteria may grow and divide in around 20 minutes. Over the course of 24 hours, a bacterium with a changed gene that offers a survival advantage can give rise to thousands of children that possess the same gene. Likewise, each new bacterium can produce thousands of offspring by the next day. As a result, a mutation can quickly spread within a bacterial population and, because the feature can be passed to unrelated bacteria, it can also spread to other bacterial communities.

Human-imposed selection pressures, such as antibiotic usage or misuse, factory-farm agriculture that crowds' animals in a limited space, and human encroachment on previously undisturbed land, are impacting microbial evolution and the onset or re-emergence of infectious illnesses.

Tip 13: Branches of Microbiology

Microorganisms may be found everywhere in nature, and they have a significant impact on other life forms such as humans, plants, and animals in a variety of ways. The impact of microorganisms on the environment can be beneficial or detrimental. These bacteria exhibit a wide variety of activity and diversity. Therefore, microbiology is further subdivided into sections based on taxonomic characteristics and the use of microorganisms in many sectors. Based on taxonomic characteristics, microbiology is further divided into different branches, i.e., bacteriology, mycology, phycology, parasitology, immunology, virology.

Tip 14: Bacteriology

Bacteriology is a subfield of Microbiology that studies bacteria. Bacteria are prokaryotic, unicellular organisms. Their multiplication method is binary fission. Bacteria can be parasitic or free-living in the environment. The nuclear material isn't attached to the nuclear membrane. This bacterium may or may not be motile. They can be rod-shaped, spiral-shaped, or cocci-shaped, and they can be aerobic, non-aerobic, or facultative anaerobic in nature. Some bacteria have an autotrophic or heterotrophic mode of nutrition based on their method of nutrition.

Tip 15: Mycology

Mycology is a field of microbiology that studies fungi. This fungus's cells are eukaryotic in nature, with the nuclear material surrounded by chitin, cellulose, or both. These fungal cells are chemoorganotrophic and non-photosynthetic in nature. These fungal cells are classified into two types: yeast and molds.

Yeast-Yeast cells might be single cells or pseudomycelium. Budding or Spore creation is the mode of reproduction. Ascomycetes are yeast cells that can be oval, rod-shaped, or spherical.

Molds-Molds grow in the form of hyphae, which are multicellular filamentous structures. This hypha might be spectated or not. They have the ability to reproduce sexually as well as asexually.

Tip 16: *Phycology*

Phycology is a subfield of microbiology that studies algae. They are eukaryotic, photosynthetic, and multicellular organisms.

Tip 17: *Parasitology*

It is a subfield of biology concerned with the study of parasites. This branch focuses on three primary groups of bacteria: parasitic protozoa, parasitic worms, and arthropods. The interaction between the host and the parasite is also investigated. These parasites can be either unicellular or multicellular. These parasites are primarily responsible for infecting people and animals.

Tip 18: *Immunology*

Immunology is a discipline of microbiology that studies the immune systems of all organisms, particularly humans and animals. The interactions between the host body, pathogens, and immunity are investigated in this discipline of microbiology.

Tip 19: *Virology*

Viruses are the subject of this field of microbiology. Viruses are extremely small ultra-microscopic organisms that may be seen under an electron microscope. Viruses are metabolically inactive and rely entirely on host cells for reproduction. Viruses may infect any sort of cell, from bacteria to humans. It only contains one form of nucleic acid, either DNA or RNA.

Applied Branches of microbiology consist of Air Microbiology, Water Microbiology, Sewage Microbiology, Soil Microbiology, Food microbiology, Milk Microbiology, Industry Microbiology, Medical Microbiology, Geomicrobiology, and Biotechnology.

Tip 20: Air Microbiology

Microorganisms move from one location to another via the air. Microorganisms are found everywhere in nature, and microorganisms in the air are responsible for food contamination and disease transmission. Infections such as TB, influenza, and several plant and animal fungal diseases, among others, spread through the air. As a result, it is critical to research a specific region in order to manage and prevent the spread of some bacteria. All studies connected to air and microbes are carried out in this discipline.

Tip 21: Water Microbiology

Water is the most vital item that a living form needs to live. As a result, the water utilized should be clean, devoid of pollutants, and free of disease-causing organisms. Municipal water purification devices are used to filter water, and water quality is monitored by water testing. In addition, water microbiology is used to determine whether or not the water is drinkable. The availability of high-quality water is critical since water can be a source of disease transmission.

Tip 22: Sewage Microbiology

Sewage water is the community's used water. This sewage water contains a variety of chemicals as well as pathogenic and non-pathogenic microorganisms. If sewage water is not treated before disposal, it can affect the environment as well as any living thing. Therefore, sewage water is treated in sewage microbiology using various procedures, chemicals, and beneficial microbes.

Tip 23: Soil Microbiology

Many microorganisms are thought to live in the soil. Soil microbiology is the study of microorganisms found in soil. If helpful microorganisms are present in the soil, it becomes productive. These microorganisms are involved in the transformation of nutrients necessary for crop growth as well as the breakdown of organic matter to its simplest form. The bacteria also aid in the fixation of atmospheric nitrogen for plant development. Antibiotic-producing microorganisms are abundant in soil; bacteria, fungus, viruses, and protozoa are among the microorganisms found in soil. As a result, studying soil microbiology is critical.

Tip 24: Food Microbiology

Food microbiology is an important branch since it studies the interactions of microorganisms with food. Microorganisms interact with food in two ways: they can ruin it and transfer infection or sickness. Second, it can use some substrate and turn it into a fermentation product. Microorganisms may ferment the substrate and produce products such as curd, idli, cheese, butter, etc. If food quality is not properly checked, it may result in the spread of foodborne illnesses. As a result, research into fermentation and food quality control is critical.

Tip 25: Milk Microbiology

Milk is rich and one of the most incredible foods, thus there is a risk of contamination. There is a high risk of milk deterioration if the milk becomes contaminated. Milk is widely employed in the dairy sector, where it is used to make a variety of products such as cheese, butter, ghee, and curd. Beneficial bacteria in milk aid in the manufacture of numerous milk products, while bad bacteria may destroy everything. Foodborne infections can spread through milk if it is not sufficiently sterile. As a result, it is critical to research milk sterilization, the creation of diverse milk products, and the prevention of milk-borne infections.

Tip 26: Industrial Microbiology

Industrial microbiology is a field of microbiology that uses microorganisms to transform huge amounts of substrate into commercially valuable products. Microorganisms are utilized on a wide scale in several businesses to produce a variety of products such as antibiotics, drinks, vaccines, proteins, and food. As a result, it is critical to research organisms that may be used in industry to produce commercially significant products.

Tip 27: Medical Microbiology

There are numerous beneficial microorganisms in nature, as well as many destructive microorganisms. Harmful in the sense that it is a disease-causing microorganism. The study of the causal agent of illness, identification, pathogenicity, prevention, and treatment of disease is carried out in this branch. It also addresses antibiotics.

Tip 28: Geomicrobiology

This branch of microbiology investigates the interactions of microbes with geological substances such as coal formation, mineral and gas formation, and mineral recovery from low-grade ores. It also aids in the breakdown of hydrocarbons that have collected in nature as contaminants. Microorganisms are employed to clean up oil spills in the water by degrading hydrocarbons and saving marine life surrounding the spill.

Tip 29: Advanced Instruments Microbiology

Clinical Microbiology, Food Microbiology, and Biotechnology rely on Advanced Instruments Microbiology products. Scientists may isolate, catch, plate, and grow organisms for diagnosis or study with the Advanced Instruments Anaerobic Jar System. Advanced Instruments focuses on a tiny subset of the various microbiological methods available.

Advanced Instruments focuses on a specific area of microbiology, such as microbial physiology, evolutionary microbiology, microbial genetics, environmental microbiology, aero microbiology, veterinary microbiology, industrial microbiology, and food microbiology. These are only a few of the research areas where Advanced Instruments, Inc. has been used to assist microbiologists in studying "germs" and bacteria. Microbiology has evolved into a broad word encompassing several sub-disciplines or fields of study.

Tip 30: Microbial Physiology

The study of microbial cell architecture, development, and metabolism operate in live creatures is known as microbial physiology. It focuses on viruses, bacteria, fungus, and parasites. It is sometimes referred to as the study of microbial cell functions, which encompasses investigating microbial growth, metabolism, and cell structure. Microbial physiology is crucial in metabolic engineering as well as functional genomics. OMICS Group International is a major Open Access Publisher that publishes 700+ peer-reviewed journals with high-quality content. Journal of Bacteriology and Parasitology is one of the leading journals that publishes high-quality articles worldwide. The Journal of Bacteriology and Parasitology covers a wide variety of topics related to bacterial and parasitic illnesses.

"Strict anaerobes play an important role in the natural geochemical cycles of carbon, nitrogen, and Sulphur." Our principal research objective is to use the activities catalyzed by these anaerobes, such as the synthesis of chemicals and fuels from waste streams. "The Microbial Physiology group investigates the physiology of anaerobic microorganisms and anaerobic microbial communities (natural or manufactured) that play a significant role or have application potential in sustainable circular economy techniques. This includes, for instance: isolating, characterizing, and applying novel anaerobes with biotechnological application potential, studying metabolic microbial interactions in natural systems (e.g., syntrophic in anaerobic digesters), and in constructed synthetic communities microbial conversions of one-carbon compounds (CO_2, CO, formate, methanol, CH_4) to added-value products, anoxic respiration with Sulphur compounds for metal recovery chemolithotrophic processes on solid surfaces, Combining cultivation methods with proteome and transcriptome analysis yields in-depth knowledge into metabolic pathways.

Tip 31: Evolutionary Microbiology

Microbial evolution is a new topic of study, but how microorganisms contribute to human health and illness beyond pathologic infections is unique. Microbes and humans coexist as an ecosystem, with microbial genes considerably outnumbering those originating from human sperm and egg. Their capacity to swiftly alter in response to environmental stimuli may have health-related impacts on their human hosts, which can be transferred vertically and result in transgenerational adaptations. We are still in the early stages of investigating the nature and significance of these interactions and how they may influence not only individual individuals and their offspring but also populations.

There are evident examples of lateral transfer, such as when viruses move genes from one species to another or insert themselves in the midst of a gene, causing significant alterations. This can muddy the picture at times, but it obviously plays a far larger part in the complexity of microbial evolution. The current sequencing of huge numbers of microbial genomes is allowing us to rapidly expand our understanding of that process, offering substantially different views of the early phases of cellular evolution and the establishment of the three kingdoms than those based largely on ribosomal RNA data. Only a fraction of the genes of the large viruses looks like anything seen to date in cellular organisms, and a significant number of similarities have been identified between genes of bacteriophages and eukaryotic viruses. There is much evidence that most virus families are quite old and have coevolved with their varied hosts.

Tip 32: Microbial Genetics

Microorganisms have the ability to acquire genes and hence conduct recombination. The mixing of genetic material from two animals leads to the formation of a new chromosome with a genotype distinct from that of the parent. New chemical or physical capabilities frequently accompany this novel gene arrangement.

Several types of recombination have been seen in microbes. The most frequent type of recombination is general recombination, which often includes a reciprocal exchange of DNA between two DNA sequences. It can occur anywhere on the microbial chromosome and is characterized by the exchanges that occur during bacterial transformation, bacterial recombination, and bacterial conjugation and transduction.

The integration of a viral genome into the bacterial chromosome is a second kind of recombination known as site-specific recombination. A third form is replicative recombination, which occurs when genetic components transfer from one location on the chromosome to another. Recombination principles apply to prokaryotic microbes but not to eukaryotic microorganisms. Eukaryotes have a complete sexual life cycle, which includes meiosis. During the process of crossing over, novel combinations of a certain gene form. This mechanism happens between homologous chromosomes and is not observed in bacteria, which have just one chromosome. Most of the work in microbial genetics has been done with bacteria, and the specific characteristics of microbial genetics are often those related to prokaryotes such as bacteria.

Tip 33: Environmental Microbiology

Environmental microbiology deals with the study of microorganisms, their interaction with each other, and with their environment as well. It consists of three primary kingdoms of life along with viruses; Eukaryota, Archaea, and Bacteria. Because of their pervasiveness, microorganisms have an influence on the entire ecosystem. Microbial life is essential for controlling biogeochemical processes in nearly all of our planet's settings, including some of the most severe, such as freezing conditions and acidic lakes, as well as those of the most familiar, such as the human small intestine. By virtue of their biomass alone, microbes provide a major carbon sink due to the quantitative enormity of microbial life (estimated as 5.0$10^{30}$ cells; eight orders of magnitude more than the number of stars in the visible universe). Aside from carbon fixation, the primary collective metabolic activities of microbes (such as nitrogen fixation, methane metabolism, and sulfur metabolism) drive global biogeochemical cycles. The vastness of microbe creation means that even in the absence of eukaryotic life, these activities would most likely continue unaffected.

Tip 34: Aero Microbiology

The study of live bacteria floating in the air is known as aero microbiology. These bacteria are known as bioaerosols (Brandl et al., 2008). Though there are many fewer microorganisms in the atmosphere than in the seas and soil, there is still a substantial number that can have an impact on the atmosphere (Amato, 2012). Once suspended in the air column, these bacteria may move large distances with the assistance of wind and precipitation, increasing the occurrence of widespread illness caused by these microorganisms. These aerosols are environmentally relevant because they have been linked to illness in people, animals, and plants. Microbes are typically suspended in clouds, where they can undertake actions that change the chemical makeup of the cloud and may even trigger precipitation and plants.

Many physical environment elements influence the launching, transit, and deposition of bioaerosols. Particles suspended in the air column are often propelled by air turbulence and originate mostly in terrestrial and aquatic habitats (Pepper 2011). Winds are the most common mode of transfer for bioaerosols. Bioaerosols can be deposited by a variety of methods, including gravity dragging them down, contact with surfaces, or mixing with rain, which draws the particles back down to the earth's surface.

Tip 35: Atmosphere

Air includes bacteria and water droplets, dust particles, and other stuff (Al-Dagal 1990). Microbes travel along a certain path when they are suspended in the atmosphere. They are first released into the air. Humans, animals, and vegetation are responsible for releasing airborne microorganisms. Al-Dagal, 1990. They are then moved (through different means such as wind, machines, and humans) and eventually placed somewhere fresh. The atmosphere can have a wide range of physical properties, including extremes in relative humidity, temperature, and radiation. These parameters have a significant effect in determining what kind of bacteria will survive in the environment and how long they will survive. They are quite severe in terms of relative humidity, temperature, and radiation.

Tip 36: Clouds

Clouds are one place where bioaerosols can be found. Cloudy water is a suspension of organic and inorganic substances in moisture (contribution of microbial activity to clouds). Clouds are not hospitable to life because germs must endure cold temperatures, the threat of desiccation, and intense UV radiation. With a pH range from 3 to 7, Clouds are likewise an acidic environment. Nonetheless, extremophile microorganisms can tolerate all of these environmental stresses. Clouds transport these germs and disperse them across large areas.

Tip 37: Physical Environment Stresses

A microbe's survival in the atmosphere is tough. The principal stress that aero microbes endure is desiccation, which restricts the length of time they can live floating in the air (Pepper 2011). Air humidity is a second component that might impact organism survival. Certain bacteria, particularly Gram + bacteria, are more tolerant of high humidity in the air, whereas Gram + cells are more tolerant of desiccation and dry environments (Pepper 2011). Temperatures must be in the middle range since too high temperatures will denature proteins, and too low temperatures can induce ice crystal formation (Pepper 2011). Finally, radiation is a possible threat to aero microbes since it may damage DNA within cells.

Tip 38: Industrial Microbiology

Industrial microbiology is a field of biotechnology that uses microbial sciences to mass-produce industrial goods, frequently employing microbial cell factories. A microorganism may be manipulated in a variety of ways to maximize product outputs. For example, it is possible to introduce mutations into an organism by exposing it to mutagens. Another method of increasing output is gene amplification, which is accomplished through plasmids and vectors. Plasmids and/or vectors are used to integrate multiple copies of a given gene, allowing more enzymes to be synthesized and, as a result, a higher product yield. The manipulation of organisms to produce a specific product has numerous real-world uses, including the manufacture of antibiotics, vitamins, enzymes, amino acids, solvents, alcohol, and everyday items. Microorganisms play an important function in the business and may be utilized in a variety of ways. For example, microbes can be employed to create antibiotics in order to treat infections. Microbes can also be useful in the food sector. Microbes are particularly beneficial in the production of several of the mass-produced items that people consume. For example, microorganisms are also used to manufacture amino acids and organic solvents in the chemical sector. Microbes can also be employed as a biopesticide in agricultural applications instead of utilizing harmful chemicals and/or inoculants to aid plant proliferation.

Tip 39: Food Microbiology

The study of microbes that hinder, generate, or contaminate food is known as food microbiology. This includes the study of microorganisms that cause food spoilage. These pathogens can cause disease (especially if food is improperly cooked or stored), microbes used to make fermented foods like cheese, yogurt, bread, beer, and wine, and microbes with other useful roles, such as producing probiotics.

Tip 40: Food safety

Food microbiology is heavily focused on food safety. Numerous pathogens and disease agents, including bacteria and viruses, are easily spread through food. Microbial toxins are potentially potential dietary hazards; nevertheless, microorganisms and their products can be employed to counteract these pathogenic germs. Probiotic bacteria can kill and inhibit pathogens, particularly those that generate bacteriocins. Purified bacteriocins, such as nisin, can also be applied directly to food items. Finally, bacteriophages, which are viruses that only infect bacteria, can be utilized to eliminate bacterial infections. Most germs and viruses are eliminated by thorough food preparation, including adequate cooking. On the other hand, toxins created by contaminants may not be able to be converted to non-toxic forms by heating or frying the contaminated food due to other safety criteria.

Tip 41: Fermentation

Fermentation is one way of preserving food and modifying its quality. Yeast, particularly Saccharomyces cerevisiae, is used to leaven bread, brew beer, and produce wine. Lactic acid bacteria, for example, are utilized in the production of yogurt, cheese, spicy sauce, pickles, fermented sausages, and delicacies such as kimchi. These fermentations have the common function of making the food product less friendly to other microbes, especially pathogens and spoilage-causing bacteria, hence increasing the food's shelf-life. Molds are also required for some cheese kinds to mature and acquire their characteristics.

Tip 42: Food Testing

Microbiological studies, such as testing for infections and spoilage organisms, are essential to verify the safety of food items. Therefore, the danger of contamination under regular user settings may be investigated, and food poisoning outbreaks can be avoided. Testing of food products and components is critical throughout the supply chain since product defects can develop at any stage of manufacturing. Microbiological tests can detect spoilage as well as evaluate germ content, yeasts and molds, and salmonella. Scientists are also developing quick and portable Salmonella detection devices capable of recognizing distinct Salmonella variations. Polymerase Chain Reaction (PCR) is a simple and low-cost method for producing several copies of a DNA fragment at a specified band ("PCR (Polymerase Chain Reaction)." As a result, scientists are utilizing PCR to detect various viruses or bacteria, such as HIV and anthrax, based on their distinct DNA sequences. Various kits are commercially available to aid in extracting nucleic acids from food pathogens, PCR detection, and differentiation. The identification of bacterial strands in food items is critical for everyone throughout the world since it aids in the prevention of foodborne diseases.

Tip 43: Chapter 1 Summary

- Micro means small, precisely up to 10^6 in size, and biology means the study of life. Microbiology refers to the study of microorganisms or microbes. Microbiology is a vast field that includes bacteriology, immunology, virology, parasitology, mycology, and other branches. A person who is a specialist in microbiology and its related topics is known as a microbiologist.
- Many microbes are helpful, while others cause infectious illnesses. Pathogenic bacteria, which often cause illnesses such as plague, TB, and anthrax, are among the species involved.
- Types and interactions of microbes are Mutualism, Competition, Commensalism, Proto-cooperation, Predation, Syntrophism, Parasitism, and Antagonism.
- Microbial evolution refers to genetically driven changes in microorganisms that persist over time. Some microbial alterations may occur as a result of selection pressure. The many changes that may occur in bacteria in response to the presence of antibiotics are the greatest illustrations of this.
- Microbiology is further subdivided into sections based on taxonomic characteristics and the use of microorganisms in many sectors. Based on taxonomic characteristics, microbiology is further divided into different branches, i.e.,

bacteriology, mycology, phycology, parasitology, immunology, and virology.
- Applied Branches of microbiology consist of Air Microbiology, Water Microbiology, Sewage Microbiology, Soil Microbiology, Food microbiology, Milk Microbiology, Industry Microbiology, Medical Microbiology, Geomicrobiology, and Biotechnology.
- Advanced Instruments focuses on a specific area of microbiology, such as microbial physiology, evolutionary microbiology, microbial genetics, environmental microbiology, aero microbiology, veterinary microbiology, industrial microbiology, and food microbiology.

Chapter 2: History

Tip 44: Early History

For many centuries before their actual discovery, the presence of microbes was speculated. Jainism, founded on Mahavira's teachings, claimed invisible microbiological life as early as the sixth century BCE. According to Paul Dundas, Mahavira claimed the presence of invisible microbiological beings dwelling in the ground, water, air, and fire. According to Jain texts, nigodas are sub-microscopic beings that live in enormous clusters and have a very brief existence. They are thought to pervade every portion of the cosmos, including plant tissues and animal flesh. Roman Marcus Terentius mentioned microbes when he warned to locate nearby homestead swamps because they contain various tiny creatures that are not visible to the naked eye. Yet, they roam in the air and are capable of invading one's body through the nose or mouth, causing serious lethal diseases.

Persian scholar Ibn Zuhr, also known as Avenzoar, suspected microorganisms' presence and articulated in his book titled "The Canon of Medicine." He was the one to find scabies mites. Another Persian scholar Al-Razi presented the first record of the occurrence of smallpox in his book "The Virtuous Life."

Girolamo Fracastoro argued in 1546 that epidemic illnesses were produced by infectious seedlike organisms that may spread infection by direct or indirect touch or vehicle transmission.

Antonie van Leeuwenhoek, who spent much of his time in Delft, Netherlands, saw bacteria and other microbes in 1676 using his own single-lens microscope. He is regarded as the father of microbiology since he pioneered the use of his own modest single-lens microscopes. While Van Leeuwenhoek is often credited as being the first to observe microorganisms, Robert Hooke made the first reported microscopic observation of mold fruiting structures in 1665. However, it has been believed that Athanasius Kircher, a Jesuit priest, was the first to observe microbes.

Kircher was one of the first to build magic lanterns for projection purposes; therefore, he must have been familiar with lens qualities. In 1646, he published "Concerning the Wonderful Structure of Things in Nature, Investigated by Microscope," arguing that "who would imagine that vinegar and milk abound with an endless multitude of worms?" He also mentioned that rotten material is teeming with crawling animalcules. In 1658, he wrote Scrutinium Pestis (Examination of the Plague), correctly saying that bacteria caused the sickness; however, what he observed was most likely red or white blood cells rather than the plague agent itself.

Tip 45: Robert Hooke

Robert Hooke was an English polymath who was a scientist and architect who was the first to observe a microorganism using a microscope. [4] As a young adult, he was a poor scientific inquirer who acquired fortune and acclaim by undertaking more than half of the architectural surveys following London's great fire of 1666. Hooke was also a member of the Royal Society, serving as its curator of experiments since 1662. Hooke was also a Geometry Professor at Gresham College.

Hooke worked as an assistant to physical scientist Robert Boyle, where he manufactured the vacuum pumps needed in Boyle's studies on gas law and conducted his own research. Hooke built the first Gregorian telescope in 1673 and then examined the rotations of Mars and Jupiter. Hooke's 1665 work Micrographia sparked interest in microscopic research. Hooke supported biological evolution by viewing minute fossils. He developed a wave theory of light while studying optics, especially light refraction. And his is the earliest documented idea of heat expanding matter, the composition of air by tiny particles at greater distances, and heat as energy.

Microscopy

Hooke's 1665 book Micrographia, which describes discoveries using microscopes and telescopes as well as original work in biology, features the first sighting of a microbe, the microfungus Mucor. Hooke invented the name cell, implying that plant structures resemble honeycomb cells. The hand-crafted, leather, and gold-tooled microscope he used to make the observations for Micrographia, originally built by Christopher White in London, is now on exhibit at Maryland's National Museum of Health and Medicine.

Hooke's, or maybe Boyle and Hooke's, views on combustion are also included in Micrographia. Hooke's investigations led him to conclude that combustion involves a material combined with air, which current scientists would agree with, but which was not commonly recognized, if at all, in the seventeenth century. Moreover, Hooke went on to establish that respiration is similarly dependent on a certain component of the air. Partington even claims that "if Hooke had continued his investigations on combustion, it is likely that he would have found oxygen."

Tip 46: Anton Van Leeuwenhoek

Antonie Philips van Leeuwenhoek was a Dutch merchant and scientist in the Golden Age of Dutch science and technology. He is renowned as "the Father of Microbiology" and was one of the earliest microscopists and microbiologists. He was entirely self-taught in science. Van Leeuwenhoek is well recognized for his pioneering work in microscopy and contributions to the scientific discipline of microbiology.

Van Leeuwenhoek opened his eyes in Delft, the Republic of Dutch. He worked as a draper until he was able to open his own store in nearly 1654. After that, he made his place in municipal politics and built a keen interest in lens making. He began to investigate the life of microorganisms with his microscope in the 1670s. In the 1590s-1720s, it was the turning point to the Golden Age of Dutch discovery and exploration.

Van Leeuwenhoek was the first to notice and experiment with microorganisms, which he first referred to as dierkens, diertgens, or diertjes (Dutch for "little creatures" [translated into English as animalcules, from Latin animalculum Meaning "tiny animal"]). He was the first to calculate their relative size. Although he saw multicellular creatures in pond water, most of the "animalcules" are regarded as unicellular organisms today. He was also the first to record microscopic observations of muscle fibers, bacteria, spermatozoa, red blood cells, gouty tophi crystals, and blood flow in capillaries. Even though van Leeuwenhoek did not produce a book, he explained his discoveries in letters to the Royal Society, which published many of his writings, and to individuals in numerous European nations.

Tip 47: Microscopic Study

Van Leeuwenhoek wanted to see the quality of the thread better than was feasible with the magnifying lenses of the period while running his draper shop. As a result, he acquired an interest in lens making, albeit there are few records of his early work. By holding the center of a short rod of soda-lime glass in front of a hot flame, one may separate the heated area to make two long whiskers of glass. The end of one whisker is then reinserted into the flame to make a very tiny, high-quality glass lens. Significantly, photos showing this lens manufacturing process's short glass stem characteristic were acquired in a May 2021 neutron tomography analysis of a high-magnification Leeuwenhoek microscope. He also created ground lenses with lesser magnifications. To help keep his methods secret, he appears to have purposefully led people to believe that grinding was his primary or sole method of lens production.

Tip 48: Francesco Redi

Francesco Redi was an Italian physician, naturalist, biologist, and poet who lived from February 18, 1626, until March 1, 1697. He is known as the "Father of Modern Parasitology" and the "Father of Experimental Biology." He was the first to refute the hypothesis of spontaneous generation by proving that maggots are produced from flies' eggs. At the age of 21, he received a doctorate in medicine and philosophy from the University of Pisa and worked in several Italy. He was a rationalist of his day and a debunker of demonstrable falsehoods such as spontaneous generation. His most renowned experiments are detailed in his magnum work, Esperienze intorno alla generazione degli insetti (Experiments on the Generation of Insects), which was published in 1668. He debunked the myth that vipers drink wine and can break glasses and that their venom is dangerous when consumed. He accurately noted that snake venom was created by the fangs, not the gallbladder, as previously thought. He was also the first to identify and describe the features of over 180 parasites, including Fasciola hepatica and Ascaris lumbricoides. He also distinguished between earthworms and helminths (like tapeworms, flukes, and roundworms). He may have invented the control, which is the foundation of experimental design in modern biology. Bacco in Toscana ("Bacchus in Tuscany"), a collection of his poems, originally published in 1685, is regarded as one of the best works of 17th-century Italian poetry and was awarded a medal of honor by Grand Duke Cosimo III.

Tip 49: *Spontaneous Generation*

Redi is most known for his series of experiments, published in 1668 as Esperienze intorno alla generazione degli insetti (Experiments on the Generation of Insects), which is regarded as his masterwork and a watershed moment in modern scientific history. The book is one of the first steps in disproving the hypothesis of "spontaneous generation," often known as Aristotelian abiogenesis. The prevalent belief at the time was that maggots developed spontaneously from decomposing flesh.

Redi arranged the six jars into two groups of three: In one experiment, he placed an unknown object in the first jar of each group, a dead fish in the second, and a raw slice of veal in the last. Redi used tiny gauze to cover the tops of the first series of jars, allowing only air to enter. He didn't close the door on the other bunch. After a few days, he noticed maggots on the objects in the open jars, where flies might settle, but not in the gauze-covered jars. The meat was maintained in three jars in the second trial. One jar was left open, while the other two were covered, one with cork and the other with gauze. Flies could only penetrate the uncovered container, and maggots emerged there. Maggots appeared on the gauze-covered gauze in the jar but did not survive.

Redi resumed his studies by trapping the maggots and waiting for them to transform into flies, which they did. Also, no maggots emerged when dead flies or maggots were placed in sealed jars with dead animals or calves; however, maggots appeared when the same thing was done with living flies. Knowing the fates of outspoken intellectuals such as Giordano Bruno and Galileo Galilei, Redi took care to present his new ideas in a way that did not violate Church theological tradition. Hence, his interpretations were always based on biblical verses, such as his famous adage: Omne vivum ex vivo ("All life comes from life").

Tip 50: Lazzaro Spallanzani

Lazzaro Spallanzani (January 12, 1729 – February 11, 1799) was an Italian Catholic priest, biologist, and physiologist who made significant contributions to the experimental study of body functioning, animal reproduction, and animal echolocation. His studies on biogenesis opened the path for the demise of the hypothesis of spontaneous generation, a prevalent belief at the time that life grows from inanimate materials. However, the ultimate nail in the coffin was delivered a century later by French scientist Louis Pasteur.

Experiencias Para Servir a La Historia De La Generación De Animales y Plantas (Experiences to Serve to the History of the Generation of Animals and Plants), published in 1786, included his most important works. Among his contributions were experimental demonstrations of ova-spermatozoa fertilization and in vitro fertilization.

Tip 51: Spontaneous Generation

In 1765, Spallanzani published Saggio di osservazioni microscopiche concernenti il sistema della generazione de' signori di Needham, e Buffon (Essay on microscopic observations concerning the generation system of Messrs. Needham and Buffon), the first systematic rebuttal of the theory of spontaneous generation. The microscope was already available to researchers at the time, and using it, the theory's proponents, Pierre Louis Moreau de Maupertuis, Buffon, and John Needham, concluded that there is a life-generating force inherent in certain types of inorganic matter that causes living microbes to create themselves if given enough time. Spallanzani's experiment demonstrated that it is not an intrinsic property of matter and can be eliminated by boiling for an hour. He argued that bacteria migrate via the air and may be eliminated by boiling since they did not reappear as long as the item remained hermetically shut. Needham contended that experiments undermined the "vegetative force" essential for spontaneous genesis. Spallanzani laid the ground for Louis Pasteur's study, which demolished the hypothesis of spontaneous generation nearly a century later.

Tip 52: Louis Pasteur

Louis Pasteur was a French scientist and microbiologist who pioneered the ideas of immunization, microbial fermentation, and pasteurization. His chemical research resulted in tremendous advancements in the knowledge of disease causation and prevention, laying the groundwork for hygiene, public health, and much of contemporary medicine. By creating rabies and anthrax vaccinations, his work is credited with saving millions of lives. He is considered as one of the pioneers of modern bacteriology and has been dubbed the "Father of Bacteriology" and the "Father of Microbiology" (a title he shares with Robert Koch, with the latter also being bestowed upon Antonie van Leeuwenhoek).

Pasteur was the one who disproved the theory of spontaneous genesis. His experiment, conducted under the auspices of the French Academy of Sciences, revealed that nothing ever formed in sterile and sealed flasks but that microbes may grow in sterilized but open flasks. In 1862, the academy awarded him the Alhumbert Prize, worth 2,500 francs, for this attempt.

Pasteur is also considered one of the forefathers of the germ theory of illnesses, a relatively new medical notion at the time. His numerous tests demonstrated that illnesses might be averted by eliminating or halting germs, thereby confirming the germ hypothesis and its therapeutic application. He is most known to the general public for developing the technique of treating milk and wine to prevent bacterial contamination, which is today known as pasteurization. Pasteur also made important discoveries in chemistry, most notably on the chemical foundation for crystal asymmetry and racemization. Early in his career, his research on tartaric acid resulted in the first resolution of what is now known as optical isomers. His study paved the groundwork for today's knowledge of a key concept in organic compound structure. Until his death, he was the director of the Pasteur Institute, which was founded in 1887, and his corpse was placed in a vault under the institute. Despite his revolutionary research, Pasteur's name got connected with a number of issues. For example, a historical examination of his diary shows that he used trickery to defeat his opponents.

Tip 53: Germ Theory of Diseases

While working at Lille, Pasteur was inspired to research fermentation. In 1856, M. Bigot, a local winemaker whose son was one of Pasteur's pupils, requested Pasteur's guidance on the challenges of generating beetroot alcohol and souring.

According to his son-in-law, René Vallery-Radot, Pasteur delivered a paper regarding lactic acid fermentation to the Société des Sciences de Lille in August 1857. Still, it wasn't seen until three months later. Then, on November 30, 1857, a memoir was published. "I intend to establish that, just as there is an alcoholic ferment, the yeast of beer, which is found everywhere that sugar is decomposed into alcohol and carbonic acid, so also there is a particular ferment, a lactic yeast, which is always present when sugar becomes lactic acid," he wrote in his memoir.

Pasteur also published on the fermentation of alcoholic beverages. It was first published in its entirety in 1858. Decomposition, according to Jöns Jacob Berzelius and Justus von Liebig, was the source of fermentation. Pasteur disproved this hypothesis, demonstrating that yeast was responsible for fermentation to make alcohol from sugar. He also proved that when a different bacterium invaded the wine, it created lactic acid, which turned the wine sour. Pasteur discovered in 1861 that when yeast was exposed to air, less sugar was fermented per portion of yeast. The Pasteur effect was named after the reduced rate of aerobic fermentation.

Pasteur's studies also revealed that the proliferation of microorganisms was to blame for the spoilage of liquids such as beer, wine, and milk. With this established, he devised a method for heating liquids such as milk to temperatures ranging from 60 to 100 °C. This destroyed the majority of the bacteria and molds that were already there. On April 20, 1862, Pasteur and Claude Bernard undertook blood and urine tests. In 1865, Pasteur invented the procedure to combat wine's "diseases." Pasteurization became popular, and it was quickly used for beer and milk.

Pasteur developed the theory that disease is caused by microorganisms that infect animals and people as a result of beverage contamination. He recommended preventing microorganisms from entering the human body, which prompted Joseph Lister to create antiseptic procedures in surgery. Pasteur wrote Etudes sur le Vin, a book on wine illnesses, in 1866, and Etudes sur la Bière, a book about beer disorders, in 1876.

Corpuscles coated silkworms treated with pébrine. Pasteur felt the corpuscles were a sign of the sickness during the first three years. In 1870, he determined that corpuscles caused pébrine (it is now known that the cause is a microsporidian). Pasteur also demonstrated that the condition was inherited. Pasteur devised a method to avoid pébrine by turning female moths into a pulp after they lay their eggs. A microscope was used to inspect the pulp, and if corpuscles were found, the eggs were killed. Pasteur determined that bacteria caused flacherie. Viruses are now assumed to be the major cause. Flacherie's spread might be accidental or inherited. Hygiene might be employed to avoid inadvertent flacherie. Moths whose digestive chambers did not contain flacherie-causing microbes were used to lay eggs, avoiding hereditary flacherie.

Agostino Bassi demonstrated that muscardine was generated by a fungus that infected silkworms in the early nineteenth century. Since 1853, two illnesses known as pébrine and flacherie have been infecting large numbers of silkworms in southern France, inflicting massive losses to farmers by 1865. As a result, Pasteur moved to Alès in 1865 and stayed for five years, till 1870.

Tip 54: *Spontaneous Generation*

Following his fermentation tests, Pasteur established that grape skin was a natural source of yeast and that sterilized grapes and grape juice never fermented. So he used sterile needles to extract grape juice from beneath the skin and wrapped grapes with sterilized linen. In both tests, wine could not be produced in sterilized containers.

His observations and thoughts contradicted the widely held belief in spontaneous genesis. Félix Archimède Pouchet, director of the Rouen Museum of Natural History, was particularly harsh in his criticism. Nevertheless, the French Academy of Sciences gave the Alhumbert Prize, worth 2,500 francs, to anyone who could empirically show for or against the idea.

Pouchet proposed that the presence of air everywhere may result in the spontaneous production of live beings in liquids. In the late 1850s, he conducted tests and claimed that the results demonstrated spontaneous creation. However, in the 17th and 18th centuries, Francesco Redi and Lazzaro Spallanzani presented evidence opposing spontaneous generation. In 1765, Spallanzani's tests revealed that bacteria were present in broths polluted by air. Pasteur replicated Spallanzani's tests in the 1860s, although Pouchet reported a different result using a different broth.

Pasteur conducted several experiments to refute spontaneous genesis. He put boiling liquid in a flask and allowed hot air to penetrate. The flask was then sealed, and no organisms developed in it. When he opened flasks containing boiling liquid in another experiment, dust entered them, allowing organisms to develop in some of them. The number of flasks in which organisms grew decreased as altitude increased, indicating that air at greater altitudes contained less dust and fewer creatures. Pasteur also utilized swan neck flasks with fermentable liquid inside. Air was allowed to enter the flask through a long curved tube, which caused dust particles to adhere to it. Nothing grew in the broths unless the flasks were tilted, causing the liquid to come into contact with the infected neck walls. This demonstrated that the live creatures that grew in such broths came from the outside, on dust, rather from spontaneously arising inside the liquid or by the influence of pure air.

These were some of the most significant tests used to disprove the hypothesis of spontaneous generation. Pasteur presented his results to the French Academy of Sciences in a series of five presentations in 1881, which were published in 1882 as Mémoire Sur les corpuscules organisées qui existent dans l'atmosphère: Examen de la doctrine des générations spontanées (Account of Organized Corpuscles Existing in the Atmosphere: Examining the Doctrine of Spontaneous Generation). In 1862, Pasteur was awarded the Alhumbert Prize. He believed that the concept of spontaneous creation would never recover from the grave blow dealt by this simple experiment. There is no known condition in which tiny organisms may have entered the planet without germs or parents who were comparable to themselves.

Tip 55: Robert Koch

The doctor and scientist Robert Koch (1843–1910) was another pivotal contributor in identifying the microbiological origins of infectious illnesses. His work was awarded the Nobel Prize (see below) on the strength of his investigations on the causative agents of carbuncle (anthrax), cholera, and tuberculosis: Koch's conceptual, methodological, and technological contributions were critical to microbiology's astonishing advance during the Golden Age. For example, Koch pioneered the notion of "pure culture," which allowed researchers to investigate each bacterium in isolation within a complicated combination. He also created a culture medium that was nutritionally comparable to the elements of physiological fluids in order to promote the development of its microorganisms.

A significant conceptual change was the solidification of the surroundings by adding gelatin to the nutritive mixes at the start and agar at the conclusion. Compared to gelatin, agar had the considerable benefit of being a cement polymer that liquefied at 100°C and did not harden until the temperature dropped below 50–60°C. The Koch school also created a simple but vital instrument for the progress of microbiology: the petri dish (named after its creator, Richard Petri), which allowed bacteria to be inoculated and cultured, replacing the uncomfortable glass plates covered with a bell jar that had previously been employed.

Koch also included coloring compounds derived from aniline, unique to bacteria staining (methylene blue, fuchsia, and crystal violet), still used in microbiology laboratories today. In addition, they produced microscopes with chromatic aberration-free lenses in partnership with the major German optical industry (Abbé and Zeiss). The advent of microphotography, which allowed Koch's school to capture and present adequate observations and findings regardless of location, was a forerunner to this effort.

As a result, when Koch assumed the job of director at the Imperial Health Office's bacteriology laboratory in Berlin, his staff was equipped to research germs as agents responsible for serious human diseases. These comprised not only accurate staining procedures, monitoring, and culture in solid settings but also sanitation and disinfection techniques and the use of incubation cases and stoves as experimental animal models.

Tip 56: Koch's Postulates

Using this fundamental analytical and technological armament, Koch launched the research of Bacillus anthracis in 1873, based on some prior data (Davaine 1868; Eberth 1872) pointing to these bacteria's causative role in anthrax. Koch isolated individual colonies of B. anthracis and successfully reproduced them in vitro using pure culture methods. In addition, his laboratory took the first microphotographs of fixed and stained preparations with methylene blue and described the parameters for the creation and germination of endospores, differentiated structures of vegetable cells with high resistance to a range of chemicals.

However, Koch's main focus at the time was to demonstrate the operational capability of the standards established by his first teacher, Jacob Henle (1809–1885), to clearly establish a patient's infectious nature. Koch used to work in his own small laboratory located outside the university, where he demonstrated the validity of different postulates that prove the presence of certain microbes in sick individuals. During his experiment, he isolated the pure culture of microbes from the host and witnessed its reproduction when transferred to the susceptible host. It verified his speculations. Koch defined the requirements in his renowned publications: Die ethiologie der Tuberkulos, which should be dubbed "The Koch-Henle postulates" in absolute rigor.

Later, Koch began his seminal research on the discovery of TB bacteria (Mycobacterium tuberculosis) and cholera bacteria (Vibrio cholerae) in India. Furthermore, he proposed the notion of distinctive biological bacterial infection, implying that a separate and unique bacterium caused each infectious disease.

The subsequent identification of novel infectious agents necessitated minor changes in the construction of the Koch-Henle postulates. T.M. Rivers expanded its applicability to viruses6 because of their characteristics as obligatory intracellular pathogens. S. Falkow developed a molecular version in 1988 with the goal of determining whether bacterial genes are capable of transmitting pathogen potential to microorganisms. Surprisingly, the Australians B.J. Marshall and J.R. Warren established indisputably that the bacterium Helicobacter pylori were the etiological agent producing peptic ulcers by strictly applying the Koch-Henle postulates. They received the Nobel Prize in 2005, exactly one century after R. Koch received it.

Tip 57: Golden Aged Microbiology

The implementation of these fundamental postulates ushered in the Golden Age of Microbiology. The Imperial Health Office's bacteriology laboratory in Berlin clearly established how certain bacteria caused severe diseases with significant morbidity and death. Simultaneously, the critical function of immunity in the prevention and treatment of severe diseases was established, supporting the development of chemotherapy, surgery, and preventive vaccinations. As a result, by the turn of the twentieth century, the causal pathogen agents of a variety of devastating pathologies had been identified, including gonorrhea (Neisser 1879), cholera (Koch 1883), diphtheria (Loeffler 1884), tetanus

(Nicolaier 1885 and Kitasato 1889), meningitis (Weichselbaun 1887), bubonic plague (Yersin 1894 (Schaudinn and Hoffman 1905).

Tip 58: Microbiologist Awarded with Nobel Prizes

It is not surprising that taking this picture into account, following the initial launch in 1901, the first designations corresponding to the so-called Nobel Prize for Physiology or Medicine were intended to reward new and capital advances in our understanding of the critical role played by microscopic organisms as causative agents of infectious diseases. In the following lines, I shall review the Nobel laureates in microbiology throughout this decade (1901–1910), stressing the major achievements that prompted the Swedish Academy to award the prize.

Tip 59: Emil Adolf von Behring

Emil von Behring (1854–1917), a microbiologist, was the first laureate to receive the Nobel Prize in 1901. After training as a military doctor in Berlin, he began his career as a surgeon in many military battles. His personal experience with injured troops, on the other hand, piqued his interest in septic infections and the action of some chemical agents that do not kill bacteria but render the poisons they release dormant. Von Behring left the army in 1889 to work as an assistant to R. Koch at Berlin's renowned Institute of Infectious Diseases. He then became a professor at the University of Halle (1894), and in 1895 he transferred to the Marburg Institute of Hygiene.

Von Behring's pioneering investigations, conducted in collaboration with the Japanese bacteriologist Shibasaburo Kitasato (1853–1931), were influential in the field of immunology. Both found that the diphtheria bacillus generated a poisonous toxin. Injection of treated serum containing the inactive toxin generated a protective state in rabbits. As a result, receptor animals should create a toxin-neutralizing chemical capable of regulating the illness (antitoxins). These advancements might be applied to other infectious illnesses such as tetanus. A critical aspect was to demonstrate the unique character of the reaction: antitoxins used to combat diphtheria did not protect against tetanus, and vice versa. These serums, which form the cornerstone of serum treatment, might be effectively used to immunize other healthy animals and people.

The conceptual significance was huge, indicating unequivocally that disease resistance is not a fundamental attribute of physiological cells but rather exists in particular and generated components of blood serum, devoid of cells. This contribution was acknowledged in the Karolinska Institute's citation, which justified his selection: "for his work on serum treatment, particularly its use to diphtheria, by which he has created a new route in the sphere of medical science."

Tip 60: Kitasato-Related Questions Fade into Oblivion.

The Nobel Prize in Physiology and Medicine award has not been without controversy since its first edition and throughout its long and broad history. But, first, consider the following fascinating question: Why did Kitasato not share the Nobel Prize with von Behring in 1901? This Japanese scientist came to Germany to work in Koch's laboratory and is credited with isolating the tetanus bacillus in pure culture, producing an anti-tetanus serum alongside von Behring, and inducing passive immunity in animals. He also worked on developing antitoxins that were successful against TB and anthrax.

In 1891, Kitasato returned to Japan and began a distinguished scientific career by co-founding the Institute for the Study of Infectious Diseases with A. von Wasserman, one of his first assistants. Among other accomplishments, Kitasato and his partner

Shiga Kioshi found the bacterium that caused bubonic plague independently of Yersin in Hong Kong and the etiological agent of dysentery. However, his omission from the first election in 1901 has sparked debate. The committee believed that Alfred Nobel's words—"the person who has made the most important discovery"—too literally. In any event, while von Behring's study on diphtheria was published alone, the critical role of the anti-tetanus serum was not realized until the onset of the First World War.

Tip 61: Ronald Ross

The European colonial powers felt obligated to examine the endemic tropical illnesses in Africa and Asia that were destroying their armies due to the microbial hypothesis of disease. Their cooperation resulted in deciphering the life cycles of pathogenic organisms, which were frequently complicated and non–bacterial in origin. In this manner, Koch identified Asian cholera in 1883, followed by the discoveries of the cause of Maltese fever (1897) and malaria (1901).

Ronald Ross (1857-1922), a British doctor, was awarded the Nobel prize in Medicine or Physiology in 1902 for his splendid work on malaria. He exposed how it enters the individual; thus laying the base for effective observations on its methods of obtaining it and the reason for the illness. Despite being born in Nepal, Ross studied medicine in London, gaining a good foundation in mathematics and biology as well as an appreciation for art and literature. He enrolled in the Indian Medical Service after failing his tests for a place in the British MRCS (1881). During this time, his commitment to study was essentially non-existent because he lived like a doctor of the British elite (i.e., playing golf, fishing, shooting, etc.). He did, however, complete his first novel, The Child of the Ocean.

Ross's research of malaria would begin during his second visit to India when he was given microscopes and microbiological gear.

This was suggested by the scientist P. Manson, who agreed with the Frenchman C. A. Laveran (see below) about the role of insects as carriers of the plague. Next, Ross addressed one of the disease's most important issues: the transmission mechanism and the emergence of symptoms. His first observations correctly identified the Anopheles mosquito as the host of malaria. Later, he proved how the sickness was transmitted by female mosquito bites, which allowed the parasite's eggs to mature using his classic bird studies. Ross then concentrated on the numerous phases of the pathogen's life cycle. A group of renowned Italian malariologists (Bignami, Bastianelli, Celli, Golgi, Grassi, and Marchiafava) independently confirmed the transmission of human malaria by mosquitos and completed the life cycle of Plasmodium falciparum.

Ross went to England and joined the Liverpool School of Tropical Medicine before moving to King's College Hospital in London. He finished his work by establishing sanitary techniques of preventive and widespread eradication efforts in southern Europe and northern Africa. It is worth noting that Ronald Ross had a high cultural and intellectual level due to his mathematical studies. He created complex models that he used in his epidemiological investigations; he also had a strong artistic bent, which led him to write novels and poetry collections. However, his later years were overshadowed by a disagreement about the source of the discoveries between Ross, his professor P. Mason, and the Italian malariologists.

Tip 62: Robert Koch

Despite all of the outstanding conceptual, systematic, and technological contributions Koch made—reviewed above—that would constitute indisputable merit that would justify the Nobel distinction from the start, it would not be until 1905 that this brilliant investigator was presented the award for his specific work on tuberculosis, as so succinctly summarized by the Karolinska Institute: "for his investigations and discoveries in relation to tuberculosis." As a result, Koch's work with the TB bacillus will be discussed more below.

Tuberculosis was one of Europe's most serious health concerns in the nineteenth century, with high death rates in major towns and mostly affecting infants, adolescents, and the elderly. When Koch took on the subject, there was already data pointing to the disease's infectious nature. However, Koch initially faced two types of difficulties: Virchow's observations related to the cause of pathology, poor functioning, and defects of organisms remained dominant. In addition, it ruled out the presence of foreign-inducing agents, unforeseen consequences of Mycobacterium tuberculosis's investigation, where it was found very difficult to grow the strain in the laboratory.

To prove his hypothesis, he remained to stick to the postulates protocol established by Koch-Henle. In this way, he was able to discover stained bacillus in sick individual's tissues after applying various stains (e.g., Brown vesuvine and methylene blue, for heating over the temperature 40oC to reduce the time, etc.) until he accomplished dying the complex strain and studied the composition of the wall of mycobacteria. This technique of staining the complex strains was later polished by introducing anilines by P. Ehrlich). Characterization of macrophages as a bacterial reservoir was also one of the achievements of Koch.

To go on with the second law of pure culture in the laboratory, Koch managed to form a complex media consisting of saline solution mixed with the inoculum extracted from the samples of ill individuals (e.g., intestinal and brain tuberculosis, bronchitis, etc.). Unfortunately, to observe the appearance of the first growth in the form of faint spots, he had to wait for ten days. However, after multiple and repeated transfers, he succeeded in obtaining numerous large colonies.

Following that, numerous guinea pigs, rabbits, and other animal species were infected with TB from patients or isolated bacilli from the laboratory. The successful infection met the conditions of the third postulate and so conclusively showed that M. tuberculosis is the bacterium responsible for this potentially fatal illness. Following the same technique, Koch's laboratory successfully isolated and identified the cholera etiological agent, developed hygienic control measures for its prevention and treatment, and purification of public water systems.

Despite his monumental accomplishment, it is crucial to emphasize Koch's huge failure in TB when, in 1890, he reported that he had discovered an efficient tuberculosis treatment known as "tuberculin." However, a series of clinical trials indicated that tuberculin did not act directly against the bacillus but rather triggered the host's defense cells, which is the basis of delayed-type hypersensitivity. This test is still used today to diagnose TB infection. Trials employing tuberculin as a therapeutic vaccination began immediately, but the results were plainly disappointing. Very few patients were healed, and tuberculin appeared to enhance bacterial spread to previously uncolonized organs in some instances.

Tip 63: Charles Louis Alphose Laveran

Charles L. A. Laveran (1845–1922) was born into a French family with a strong military pedigree and studied medicine at Paris and Strasburg. He earned his doctorate in 1867 with a thesis on nerve regeneration. In 1870, he served as a military medic in Metz during the Franco–Prussian War. In 1874, he accepted a job as a professor of illnesses and epidemiology at the School of Val-de-Gráce, a position formerly held by his father. He developed an active teaching career.

Laveran was dispatched to Algeria as a military doctor in 1878 and lasted until 1883. Malaria was a true pandemic at the time, and Laveran began to investigate the black corpuscles that appeared in the blood of sick individuals. He detected a small parasite in all of the patients and thought it was the etiological culprit, first labeling it Haemamoeba laverani. As is frequently the case, the scientific community reacted with skepticism to the discovery. However, its veracity was verified years later by many malariologists. R. Ross focused on Laveran's efforts to support the parasite's transmission mechanism.

Laveran retired from the army in 1897 and joined the Pasteur Institute, where he focused on tropical illnesses such as trypanosomiasis, Sporozoa, and African sleeping sickness. He was awarded the Nobel Prize in 1907 "in appreciation of his study on the role of protozoa in disease transmission." Half of the award money was donated to the Pasteur Institute by him.

We must also acknowledge the amazing work of Cuban scientist Carlos J. Finlay on the subject of disease transmission via vector mosquitoes (yellow fever). Both Laveran and Ross acknowledged his contributions and endorsed his candidacy.

Tip 64: Paul Ehrlich and Ilya Mechnikov

In 1908, the German doctor Paul Ehrlich (1854–1915) and Ilya Mechnikov (1845–1916), a scientist of Ukrainian descent who had moved to France, were awarded the second joint Nobel Prize in Medicine (after that awarded in 1906 to Golgi and Ramón y Cajal). Their merits were too succinctly justified: "In honor of their work on immunity." However, the recognized contributions had transcendental ramifications of a scientific and clinical order that were impossible to predict within the setting of that historical period, as did Prof. K. Horner, Karolinska's rector. Horner accurately stated in a remarkable speech in celebration of the two winners that avoiding these infectious illnesses was the greatest problem faced by modern medicine at the beginning of the twentieth century. He suggested two lines of action: I find and kill the pathogen agents responsible for the sickness (which was being done), and (ii) provide the body with the required strength to resist their attacks. Because Ehrlich and Mechnikov made unique contributions, their work will be described individually.

Tip 65: Paul Ehrlich and Immunity

Ehrlich was born in the German province of Silesia (which now belongs to Poland). He studied medicine at many institutions (Breslau, Strasburg, and Freiburg) and earned his doctorate at the University of Leipzig with a thesis on the aniline staining of animal tissue. He established a suitable method for staining TB bacillus, which served as the foundation for the following changes made by Ziehl and Neelsen and is still used today as "staining of acidic–alcohol resistance." Koch personally offered Ehrlich a post as an investigative assistant in 1890. Because of his secure job, he was able to begin his fundamental research on immunity. Ehrlich demonstrated how particular toxin-antitoxin interactions are accelerated by heat and retarded by cold due to their chemical nature. In conjunction with von Behring, he developed a way to standardize the precise quantity (measured in units) of antitoxins in saline solution, laying the groundwork for future serum typification processes and their widespread usage in diagnostic tests. His immunological research enabled Ehrlich to develop his pivotal "side-chain hypothesis," which explains the unique immune response and antibody formation.

Tip 66: The Magic Bullet

Ehrlich traveled to Frankfurt in 1899, when he launched a new key area of research, a forerunner of contemporary chemotherapy, described as the treatment of infectious disorders with synthetic chemical substances. Ehrlich revived an ancient theory of the unique feature of chemically employed medications, the composition of which had to be investigated in connection to their mode of action and affinity for cells of the organism against which they were aimed. His goal was to find chemical compounds with a high affinity for such infections while remaining harmless to the host organism and capable of protecting their cellular integrity (selective toxicity). Ehrlich dubbed these unusual chemicals "magic bullets."

His laboratory tried a variety of chemicals, but just a handful of them were successful. Finally, despite certain side effects such as ocular atrophy, the oxide of arsenic (atoxyl) was a notable success against the spirochaete that caused syphilis. This accomplishment sparked a new method based on the chemical synthesis of arsenicals with the goal of creating safer and more efficient derivatives for treating syphilis, culminating in 1910 with the discovery of the renowned salvarsan (composed 606 of all the analyzed series).

Furthermore, Ehrlich pioneered the introduction of new concepts and approaches that were critical in chemotherapeutic research. 16 For example, screening involves the simultaneous sampling of a large number of potentially interesting compounds, or the synthesis of a collection of variant molecules from a substance with significant antimicrobial activities, intending to boost its power while decreasing its toxicity. In addition, Ehrlich demonstrated the metabolic activation process that some medicines go through inside the body while staying inert in vitro. 15 Furthermore, during his early study on trypanosomes, he discovered that it was impossible to entirely eliminate the bacteria after treatment with trypan and atoxyl. He raised the issue of microbial resistance to chemotherapeutics.

Tip 67: *Ilya Mechnikov and Phagocytosis*

Mechnikov was born in Kharkov (Ukraine), where he excelled as a student, graduating with honors in natural sciences. Later, he would tour other German institutions (Göttingen and Munich) before returning to Russia and being appointed professor of zoology at the University of Odessa in 1870.

Mechnikov's life took a drastic turn when he traveled to Messina to pursue his prior research into comparative embryology. He researched starfish larvae and, subsequently, Daphnia, a freshwater crustacean, noticing the existence of mobile cells that assault the spores of different dangerous fungi, deducing that they may act as part of these species' defensive mechanism.

Mechnikov established his general theory of phagocytosis in 1884, which he defined as the ability of certain specialized cells (mostly the leucosis) to safeguard the organism's integrity by consuming and killing germs and other foreign particles. He proposed that phagocytosis was a universal process that had been sufficiently developed in the biosphere and had been conserved throughout evolution. Mechnikov went back to Odessa and attempted to introduce Pasteur's rabies vaccine. However, he encountered tremendous antagonism from the local populace, partly due to the fact that he was not a doctor. As a result, he moved to Paris from Odessa in 1888. Pasteur provided him a laboratory and a permanent post in the future Pasteur Institute, where Mechnikov remained, rising to the vice director for the remainder of his life.

He conducted substantial research on the transmission mechanisms of syphilis and its treatment in collaboration with Roux (introducing certain techniques that Ehrlich later used). He was particularly interested in the microflora found in the human colon, developing a novel notion that senility was caused by the buildup of metabolites and waste products generated by enteric bacteria. Mechnikov also had a significant career as a scientific writer and thinker, publishing two volumes of The Comparative Pathology of Inflammation in 1892, which significantly impacted the scientific world.

Tip 68: Golden Era of Antibiotics

Every antibacterial antibiotic developed, regardless of chemical class or mode of action, has resulted in resistance in the target microorganisms. The World Health Organization describes resistance as a "rising danger," and the human consequences of antibacterial drug resistance throughout the world are staggering: 23 000 fatalities per year in the United States. Despite this threat, new medication discoveries have been delayed in the previous 50 years, particularly for broad-spectrum and Gram-negative antibiotics. For example, only two novel types of systemic antibacterial medicines (oxazolidinones and lipopeptides) were released into Europe between the 1970s and 2009. This slump persists despite the rise in genetic sciences, target-based high-throughput screening technologies, and breakthroughs in rational medication design. It is hardly unexpected that several authors are advocating for a return to effective tactics of the past, although in a more modern form. This brief assessment of early successful antibacterial drug development methodologies should give hope and evidence for a return to natural product-based antibacterial screening.

Tip 69: Synthetics and Early Days

Antibacterial drug research has a lengthy history, and one of the first antibacterial medications was found by Paul Ehrlich, who worked with tiny compounds to discover a "silver bullet" against syphilis. He was aware that the arsenic chemical 'atoxyl' had been effective against trypanosomes and avian spirochetes, so when the spirochete Treponema pallidum was discovered to cause syphilis, his team began synthesizing and testing derivatives using an early high-throughput approach. Compound 606, or salvarsan, produced great results against T. pallidum and was successful in human studies conducted in 1909. Further derivatization to increase the drug's safety resulted in compound 914, 'neosalvarsan,' and the two medicines were widely used in clinics until the arrival of penicillin. These antibacterial agents inspired Gerhard Domagk. He began testing azo compounds in murine models, which led to the development of 'prontosil.' The main component of prontosil was discovered to be a sulfonamide group. So, the sulfonamide family of medications was established. These early medications laid the groundwork for a straightforward, methodical approach to synthetic drug development, but they were shortly eclipsed by the discovery of the natural substance penicillin.

Tip 70: The Natural Product Boom is Formed

In the 1920s, a laboratory's culture plates of Staphylococcus sp. got infected by airborne germs. One contaminant developed into a huge mold colony, which lysed Staphylococcus sp. colonies. Subcultures of this mold, identified as a species of Penicillium sp., were cultured in broth; the resulting mold broth filtrates were dubbed 'penicillin.' When evaluated using agar diffusion and broth dilution procedures, the filtrates showed minimal toxicity and potential antibacterial efficacy against a limited range of microorganisms. While this was not the first time an antibacterial agent was identified in a microorganism, it was possibly the most significant. By the 1940s, penicillin had been well studied and was already in widespread clinical usage. Fleming's combination of serendipity and simple but efficient antimicrobial test techniques set the door for a new era in the battle against bacterial infections.

Tip 71: An Antibacterial Drug Discovery

Waksman and Woodruff were inspired by Dubos, who had just proven the antibacterial activity of an antibiotic isolated from a soil bacterium, to expand on Fleming's work. Soil sample suspensions were cultured with bacteria, and colonies were separated for pure growth when clearings were seen. In one early experiment, a percentage of broth culture filtrate from an isolated 'Actinomyces sp.' was shown to have outstanding antibacterial activity. Actinomycin, as it was designated, was one of the earliest antibacterial drugs generated from actinomycetes and the first to be isolated in crystalline form. Waksman and colleagues found the therapeutically significant antibiotic streptomycin using the same methods.

These accomplishments resulted in the 'Waksman platform,' the most effective antibacterial drug development platform, and the beginning of the 'golden period.' The platform paved the way for our most important antibiotic classes, including tetracycline, chloramphenicol, neomycin, erythromycin, vancomycin, kanamycin, rifamycin, and gentamicin. In addition, the methodical manner of screening set this platform distinct from Fleming's work. For roughly 20 years, researchers were able to work their way through organisms (primarily actinomycetes), mining new antibacterial compounds until old hits began to re-emerge and the platform became outdated.

While natural products were thriving, only a few synthetic medications (e.g., isoniazid) were found, largely through species-specific screening against pathogens such as Mycobacterium TB. While interest in the Waksman platform began to diminish in the 1960s, hopes remained high until scientists produced the synthetic 'nalidixic acid.' Unfortunately, this optimism was short-lived since once it was optimized to produce the effective fluoroquinolones, it produced relatively few successful synthetics and no new broad-spectrum antibacterial medicines.

Tip 72: The End of an Era and New Hope

New 'high-tech' platforms were born as a result of advances such as the sequencing of the bacterial genome, subsequent genomics, rational drug design, and the development of target-based high-throughput screening methods, based on the premise that prokaryote targets could be identified and compounds that targeted them. Great expectations were placed on new approaches, but experience and time would reveal that they would mainly fail, as seen by the scarcity of novel antibacterial agents in recent decades. The failure of these new approaches has been attributed to a variety of factors, including the following: vital bacterial enzymes identified in targeted screens may not be druggable, some compounds are not testable in vitro, compound libraries are unlikely to contain the complexity that natural product antibacterial agents possess, and difficulties in identifying compounds with high affinity to protein targets while also penetrating prokaryote cell walls. Complicating matters, the Lipinski' rule of five' (created to aid in the discovery of novel medications) was widely used by businesses as a filter in high-throughput screening: a problem because effective antibacterial treatments frequently violated these guidelines.

A number of academics have recently shifted their focus from developing ever more "advanced" and sophisticated technology to mining diverse natural product sources. For example, Actinomycetes-derived antibacterial chemicals have recently been discovered in marine ecosystems such as mangrove soils and plants, as well as marine sediments. In addition, previously uncultured soil bacteria are helping to generate possibly innovative drugs such as teixobactin. Plants, too, hold promise, and a number of academics have concentrated on flora, particularly traditional and ancient plant remedies.

Tip 73: Chapter 2 Summary

- Microbes were mentioned by the Roman Marcus Terentius Varro when he warned against locating a homestead near swamps "because there are bred certain minute creatures which cannot be seen by the eyes, which float in the air and enter the body through the mouth and nose and thus cause serious diseases."
- Antonie van Leeuwenhoek, who spent much of his time in Delft, Netherlands, saw bacteria and other microbes in 1676 using his own single-lens microscope. He is regarded as the father of microbiology since he pioneered the use of his own modest single-lens microscopes.
- Robert Hooke made the first reported microscopic observation of mold fruiting structures in 1665. However, it has been believed that Athanasius Kircher, a Jesuit priest, was the first to observe microbes.
- Kircher was one of the first to build magic lanterns for projection purposes; therefore, he must have been familiar with lens qualities.
- Van Leeuwenhoek was the first to calculate their relative size. Although he saw multicellular creatures in pond water, most of the "animalcules" are regarded as unicellular organisms today. He was also the first to record microscopic observations of muscle fibers, bacteria, spermatozoa, red blood cells, gouty tophi crystals, and blood flow in capillaries.
- Actinomycetes-derived antibacterial chemicals have recently been discovered in marine ecosystems such as mangrove soils and plants, as well as marine sediments.
- Uncultured soil bacteria are helping to generate possibly innovative drugs such as teixobactin. Plants, too, hold

promise, and a number of academics have concentrated on flora, particularly traditional and ancient plant remedies.

Chapter 3: Applications of Microbiology

Tip 74: Introduction

The history of humanity's adoption of biotechnological methods is complicated by the history of microbiology as a science. The earliest evidence of the employment of microbes for cereal grain fermentation to generate an alcoholic beverage came from genetic data from the Neolithic settlement of Jiahu in China, which dates back to 7000 BC. Similar evidence was discovered in northern Mesopotamia's Zagros Mountains dated from 5400–5000 BC. The discovery of tartaric acid in an antique jar, also dated to 5400–5000 BC, at the Neolithic site of Tepe in Mesopotamia, and grape juice remains, found at Dikili Tash in Greece and dated to 5000 BC, are the earliest indications of wine manufacture. This evidence suggests that the technical technique utilized by these civilizations enabled large-scale wine manufacturing to begin approximately 5000 BC.

The Egyptians, who had previously utilized yeast to manufacture beer, began to use this bacterium to make bread. Samples were discovered at several archaeological sites dating from 2000 to 1200 BC. The foundation and spread of fermentation techniques throughout Asia, Mesopotamia, Egypt, and the Old World are characteristics of empirical domestication of yeasts, which eventually sparked Louis Pasteur's interest in identifying the real cause of fermentation.

On the other hand, technological Microbiology began to attract market interest when items derived from microbial activity became required on a large scale. This occurred during World War I, with the demand for glycerol in the creation of explosives, and in the

1940s, with the large-scale production of penicillin, discovered by Fleming.

The American economic expansion triggered by the conclusion of WWII, dubbed as the Golden Age of Capitalism, as well as the developing understanding of microbial genetics at the time, drove the formation of microorganism-based industrial processes, sparking contemporary Technological Microbiology. However, Technological Microbiology is said to have started in the 1980s, after the United States Supreme Court permitted the patenting of a Pseudomonas putida variety that is successful in the organic digestion of chemicals present in crude oil spills. Ananda Chakrabarty's request for a patent on a genetically modified bacterium contributed to a biotechnology revolution that resulted in the issue of thousands of patents, the formation of hundreds of new firms, and the production of thousands of bioengineering and food plants.

The genetic alteration of Escherichia coli in the 1970s enabled the manufacturing of artificial insulin, the first product generated by recombinant DNA technology and authorized by the US Food and Drug Administration in 1982. Over time, the selection of improved microbial strains and the manipulation of other microorganisms to obtain products to meet human demands became more common. As a result, Technological Microbiology has evolved into a science that is primarily applied to several branches of production, including food, chemical, agricultural, and pharmacological.

As a result, we have witnessed a recent advancement in Classical Microbiology, from the discovery of novel species to the selection and enhancement of current strains to the insertion of non-native genes for the acquisition of expressed products or new functional features. Therefore, although many of its fields overlap, we divided this complex and applied microbiology into six areas to facilitate our discussion: Technical Materials Microbiology, Technical Medical Microbiology, Technical Environmental Microbiology, Technical Fuel and Chemical Microbiology, Technical Agricultural Microbiology, and Technical Food Microbiology as follows.

Tip 75: *Food Technological Microbiology*

Despite the use of biotechnological techniques in the food-processing and agroindustry prior to the technological advances of the 1970s, the current trend includes the use of genetically modified microorganisms or even the use of enzymes, dyes, and other compounds derived from microbial metabolism with the goal of improving productivity, enhancing organoleptic characteristics, or even attributing new nutritional functions to certain foods. As a result, microorganisms may play two distinct functions in modern food production. First, they serve as starters in fermentations. Second, they serve as factories for the manufacture of food ingredients. In this situation, the bacterium may be genetically engineered, but it will never actively participate in the food fermentation process. In this situation, the microbes play a secondary role.

Genetic engineering has been utilized to improve the performance of yeast and natural yeast in the fermentation process. In the future, higher-quality bread and pasta will be available in less time. Yeasts have been developed to tolerate temperature and pH fluctuations and grow with high yield on a variety of substrates. Proline and trehalose, two compounds involved in stress tolerance in yeasts, are attractive candidates for the generation of resistant strains. Thus, yeasts treated to novel processes such as UV radiation have enabled the development of foods with novel nutritional properties, such as higher vitamin D levels.

A variety of microbial enzyme compositions have been tested in food processing. Amylases derived from Aspergillus niger cultures, for example, have been employed instead of chemical additives in the treatment of wheat flour, enhancing dough preparation for baking and permitting the purchase of pre-cooked dishes. Extracellular lipases, which aid in enzyme recovery, have been discovered to be particularly promising in A. niger and Rhizomucor miehei strains. These microbial lipases are used to improve the aromatization of dairy products by hydrolyzing milk fat. They can also improve the flavor of drinks and the quality of margarine and mayonnaise. Cellulases and pectinases, which are particularly useful in juice clarifying and viscosity reduction, may also be easily extracted from cultures of filamentous fungi that degrade plant biomass, such as Cladosporium sphaerospermum and Penicillium chrysogenum. Furthermore, the method for immobilizing these enzymes in prefabricated supports or polymer matrices increases their stability, activity, and selectivity, allowing them to be used and reused in industrial reactors for extended periods.

Tip 76: Agricultural Technological Microbiology

Recently, the focus on microorganisms has shifted to pesticide chemicals, namely herbicidal, insecticidal, and nematicidal. The first commercially licensed mycoherbicide was a suspension of Phytophthora palmivora chlamydospores to control Morrenia odorata (McRae, 1988), and numerous more plant parasites and phytotoxin-producing microbial species have subsequently been found. Colletotrichum gloeosporioides (Penz) Sacc. f. sp. aeschynomene can cause anthracnose symptoms in Aeschynomene virginica, hence suppressing this rice and soybean weed. Puccinia canaliculata, on the other hand, can suppress yellow nutsedge by entirely preventing flowering and limiting tuber production. On the other hand, bioherbicides have not been widely used for weed management in agronomic and horticultural crops because they have a variety of criteria, such as perfect humidity levels, that reduce their efficiency compared to conventional herbicides.

Biotechnological breakthroughs will most likely reverse this condition and increase the performance of bioherbicides in the future.

Much progress has been made in the research and marketing of bionematicides in recent years. Avermectins, which are metabolites produced by the bacteria Streptomyces avermitilis, are examples of this. These insecticides serve as models since they are non-toxic to mammals and efficacious against nematodes even at extremely low concentrations. Thus, filtrates of B. firmus cultures cause paralysis and death in adult nematodes and larvae such as Radopholus similis, Meloidogyne incognita, and Ditylenchus dipsaci, suggesting that toxic metabolite production is involved in pest management. In addition, Myrothecium verrucaria, when grown in bioreactors, seem to produce toxic metabolites which kill matured nematodes when they come in contact. Not only this, but it also prevents egg hatching and development. On the other hand, endospores of the bacteria Pasteuria sp. show parasitism as a means of control.

On the other hand, endophytic microbes invade plant tissues without causing disease symptoms, creating a stable long-term association with the host plant. Furthermore, endophytes create bioactive compounds during the encounter, which may improve the plant's fitness. Endophytic growth promotion may be caused through nitrogen fixation, phytohormone production, biocontrol of phytopathogens by the manufacture of antibiotics or siderophores, nutrient competition, and the generation of systemic disease resistance. However, characterization and bioprospection of these kinds of microbes are linked with the most diversified plant species, aiming not just to identify species that secret metabolites with the ability to synthesize antibiotics, as well as a source for collecting important biotechnological chemicals but also achieving vital agronomical strains.

Tip 77: Chemical and Fuel Technological Microbiology

Obtaining compounds such as organic acids by microbial action is highly promising, especially if the carbon supply is renewable. Most organic acids are natural products or intermediates of microbial metabolism found in key metabolic pathways. These acids, such as acetic, citric, lactic, and succinic acid, are particularly important as raw materials for the chemical or food industries due to their functional groups. Citric acid, for example, has been mandated on the market for use as a food additive, and all yearly global industrial-scale production is accomplished by the fermentation of glucose, beet molasses, cane molasses, or corn starch using A. niger. On the other hand, 100% of the world's lactic acid output is derived from microbial fermentation. This acid and its derivatives are widely utilized in the culinary, pharmaceutical, leather, and textile sectors.

Furthermore, due to the rising demand for innovative biomaterials such as biodegradable goods and biocompatible polylactics, lactic acid fermentation technologies have lately attracted increased attention. The most frequent way for producing this acid is to culture Lactobacillus spp. in whey. However, it can be produced by the activity of Rhizopus sp. under aerobic conditions in a glucose-rich medium with restricted nitrogen and through the fermentation of Saccharomyces cerevisiae in glucose- and cane juice-based media. Microbiological procedures for generating a range of organic acids are projected to become competitive, market-established and allow for an annual rise in the production of these compounds in the future.

One of the first large-scale commercial fermentation processes to reach worldwide relevance was the microbial manufacture of acetone and butanol, which was efficiently accomplished by the genus Clostridium. Still, this production has been losing ground to chemical synthesis. Similarly, the inability to compete with chemical synthesis from petrochemical feedstocks influenced the centennial microbial synthesis of glycerol. However, in a context in which the cost of propylene grew due to its limited availability, particularly in developing nations, glycerol became an essential raw material for the manufacturing of numerous chemicals, making its alternative synthesis via fermentation more appealing.

This chemical synthesis using microbial metabolic processes addresses an important need to lessen reliance on fossil fuels for energy generation. In addition, renewable resources such as waste products and biomass are transformed into a compound that is susceptible to microbial action in today's biorefineries. Therefore bio-based chemicals have gained interest and have been renewed because the transitioning environmental problems and climate change have swayed the industries far from the consumption of fossil fuel and leading towards renewable raw materials.

Microorganisms have also been investigated for their possible use in manufacturing a new generation of biofuels. Some nations now produce second-generation ethanol, for example, from lignocellulosic biomass, while improvements are still needed to make the process commercially viable. Recent discoveries, such as identifying functional xylose isomerases, have led to the production of novel yeasts capable of digesting both 5-carbon (C5) and 6-carbon (C6) sugars. In first-generation fermenters, co-fermentation of C5 sugars with cane juice can result in up to 37% more ethanol. Tolerance to acetic acid is another issue that must be addressed to produce second-generation ethanol effectively. This acid is one of the most important lignocellulose hydrolysate inhibitors. The polygenic foundation of the high acetic acid tolerance seen in some S. cerevisiae strains remains unclear. Still, its identification may lead to more efficiency in enhancing acetic acid tolerance in strains without negatively impacting other industrially significant yeast traits. However, in addition to yeast genetic enhancements, the prospection of new cellulose sources, such as forestry and agriculture wastes, and the development of pretreatment methods can help boost second-generation ethanol output.

The assumption is that bioga will provide at least 25% of all bioenergy in the future; thus, research that aims to improve the methanogenesis process or explain the structure of microbial communities has been promoted. Metagenomic methods combined with next-generation sequencing (NGS) techniques will aid in unraveling the variety of natural communities as well as communities in biogas fermenters. However, research has revealed that the majority of the microorganisms isolated from the reactors remain undiscovered and might be a source of new goods and services in the future.

Tip 78: Environmental Technological Microbiology

In solid waste composting processes, a wide range of microorganisms have been identified, including heterotrophic or autotrophic aerobic bacteria, actinomycetes, fecal coliforms, and thermophiles, as well as yeasts and other fungi. Many factors influence the microbial community present during composting. Still, the temperature is the most important element under aerobic circumstances, influencing not only the microbial kinds but also the species diversity and metabolic rate. On the other hand, the direct use of microbial enzymes in the treatment of effluents, particularly industrial effluents, has been promoted since the enzymatic activity is quicker and eliminates the need for the fermentative process. Lipases, for example, are utilized in the treatment of triglyceride-rich wastewater. These enzymes in activated sludge and other aerobic degradation processes are critical for the constant clearance of fat layers that accumulate on the surface of aerated tanks to facilitate oxygen transfer. Currently, research efforts have concentrated on combining the treatment of solid wastes or even wastewater with the use of microbial fuel cells (MFC), which are microbial cells that employ electrons given by low-value organic substrates found in trash to create energy. This alternative method employs mixed MFC cultures that are adaptable to a broad range of substrates and provides the combined benefit of wastewater treatment and energy generation.

Efforts have also been made in research to improve the filtration of drinking water. A modern biotechnological procedure known as biologically active carbon (BAC) is extremely effective in eliminating water pollutants. Microbial cells colonize the surface of the granular activated carbon (GAC) employed in the filtering mechanism throughout this procedure. As a result, significant quantities of dissolved organic matter and pollutants trapped in the GAC pores can be degraded by the biofilm produced. Furthermore, the BAC biofilm has the ability to biodegrade cyanotoxins and organic compounds that can alter the taste and odor of drinking water.

Waste treatment based on enzymatic processes is less expensive; nevertheless, the enzymes are biodegradable, and further research and prospection of thermostable or resistance to high pH fluctuations are required. The use of enzymes in waste treatment has also been hampered by a lack of understanding about the enzyme-producing species that may be useful in the process, given that only around 2% of the world's microorganisms have been evaluated as enzyme suppliers. Cell genetic manipulation, heterologous gene expression, and genetic improvement are expected to help increase enzymatic biosynthesis in microbes of interest. It can also aid in the development of the microbe's bio-factories for vital enzymes that play their role not only for environmental applications but also for industry or food; therefore, widening the substitutes for the elimination of waste products that have accumulated in water and soil historically.

Tip 79: Medical Technological Microbiology

Microorganisms' involvement in the manufacture of medical products or services has four unique aspects: (1) disease biocontrol, (2) vaccine production, (3) antibiotic production, and (4) biotherapeutic production (hormones, biomaterials, and others). These issues will be addressed during the course of this workshop.

The difficulty of adopting public strategies to prevent the spread of parasite vectors such as those of the genera Aedes and Anopheles is a recurrent issue in developing nations. Recent epidemic outbreaks of emerging and reemerging illnesses, on the other hand, have fueled the development of biotechnological approaches that can not only aid in diagnosis but also act as options for reducing transmission. For example, bacteria "Wolbachia" is introduced to the mosquito "Aedes aegypt" as an endosymbiont, which transmits illness, e.g., chikungunya, dengue, yellow fever, have known to recently discovered "Zika virus." It is one of the best examples.

The emphasis of this method is on decreasing mosquito lifetime rather than on increasing mosquito number. The presence of bacteria shortens the mosquito's life, reducing the probability of dengue virus transmission because only mature females can spread the virus. Female mosquito survival was reduced in mosquitos having the Wolbachia strain compared to mosquitos not possessing the strain. These germs are passed on from the mother to her children vertically. The bacteria manipulate their host in a variety of ways to ensure this transmission, including feminization, male death, parthenogenesis, and cytoplasmic incompatibility. Fertilization of females not infected with Wolbachia by infected men leads to embryonic death in cytoplasmic incompatibility. Females infected with the bacteria, on the other hand, will produce the greatest number of viable offspring, increasing the number of infected people in the community. Wolbachia multiplication and persistence in wild populations are aided by cytoplasmic incompatibility.

Simultaneously, the technical race for the creation of a dengue vaccine continues. The first dengue vaccine, recombinant yellow fever-17D-dengue virus (live, attenuated, and tetravalent), was recently approved for use in people aged 9–45 in Mexico, Brazil, the Philippines, El Salvador, and Paraguay. This is a vital complement to the other strategies that mostly focus on vector control. Unfortunately, however, this vaccination is now only available through private health care systems at exorbitant rates.

The word 'biobetter' has recently been used to describe next-generation therapeutic macromolecules with a more effective drug delivery mechanism. Chemical and/or engineering procedures employing molecular biology techniques are used to modify these macromolecules to improve their pharmacological qualities, such as increased activity, greater stability, fewer side effects, and reduced immunogenicity. Compared to standard biopharmaceutical versions, bio betters are far more expensive because of the need for original research and development and recent alternate administration routes, e.g., breathed formulations and dermatological applications to reduce biological instability. In the near future, the protein engineering technique's popularity, specifically site-directed mutagenesis (SDM), causes the elimination, insertion, or substitution of one or more amino acids in a given protein sequence. Therefore, it is expected to access less expensive bio-betters, a rapidly emerging biopharmaceutical class.

Tip 80: Materials Technological Microbiology

Biotechnological techniques in microbiology have also resulted in a wide range of biomaterials and biosensors. Biomaterials are manufactured or natural compounds that may operate in biological systems and are often generated by microorganisms under various environmental circumstances (tissues or organs). Biosensors combine microorganisms with a physical transducer to produce a detectable signal proportional to the analyte concentration, enabling the quick and accurate detection of analytical targets in different sectors such as food processing, medicine, environmental monitoring, and many more others.

Bioplastics are an important class of biomaterials. Polyesters that accumulate intracellularly in microorganisms in the form of storage granules and have physicochemical qualities comparable to petrochemical plastics are known as bioplastics. However, depending on the microbial origin of the bioplastic, these qualities, and the monomeric composition can be varied, and the major interest in these polymers is in their biodegradability and biocompatibility. Bioplastic can also be created as a result of biorefinery by acidogenic fermentation or pyrolysis of lignocellulosic biomass or as a consequence of biotreatment of solid or liquid wastes.

Tip 81: Other Considerations

Because microorganisms constitute the most biodiverse class, we anticipate that the appearance and dissemination of novel human and/or agricultural diseases will change from a catastrophic situation exacerbated by globalization to a recurring condition at various intervals in the future. As a result, we believe that policies aimed at epidemic control and the advancement of agricultural pests should be considered globally. There is a need to study functional traits and ecological niches in order to halt the movement of microbes from a position of species, with incalculable consequences for health and the economy. We must deal with the recurrence of illnesses and the advent of superbugs as public health emergencies that necessitate immediate decision-making. These decisions must be taken while taking into account the complete technical framework now accessible, including transgenic and recombinant DNA to create incentives for microbiological research to be translated into goods and services for society.

Tip 82: Chapter No 3 Summary

- Microorganisms may play two distinct functions in modern food production. First, they serve as starters in fermentations. Second, they serve as factories for the manufacture of food ingredients. In this situation, the bacterium may be genetically engineered, but it will never actively participate in the food fermentation process. In this situation, the microbes play a secondary role.
- Genetic engineering has been utilized to improve the performance of yeast and natural yeast in the fermentation process. In the future, higher-quality bread and pasta will be available in less time. Yeasts have been developed to be tolerant of temperature and pH fluctuations and grow with high yield on a variety of substrates.
- Moreover, flavorings for foods and natural scents were obtained with the aid of microbial enzymes despite the fact that these compounds can directly be obtained from the normal general metabolism of filamentous fungi such as Pycnoporus cinnabarinus and niger work together in a process involved in the production of vanillin. Vanillin is an important food flavoring agent.
- Obtaining compounds such as organic acids by microbial action is highly promising, especially if the carbon supply is renewable. Most organic acids are natural products or intermediates of microbial metabolism found in key metabolic pathways. These acids, such as acetic, citric, lactic, and succinic acid, are essential as raw materials for the chemical or food industries due to their functional groups.
- Biotechnological techniques to microbiology have also resulted in a wide range of biomaterials and biosensors. Biomaterials are manufactured or natural compounds that may operate in biological systems and are often generated by

microorganisms under various environmental circumstances.

Chapter 4: Research

Titled: Food Safety Knowledge, Attitudes, Practices and Incidence of *Listeria monocytogenes* in Food Products available from University Cafeterias.

Tip 83: Abstract

An abstract is a kind of summary of the whole article; it includes major points from the introduction, methodology, results, and discussion. It is ideal to have a one-page abstract.

Abstract:

During this project, a microbiological evaluation of ready-to-eat food products from four university/street food locations in Islamabad was conducted to determine their microbiological quality. The collaborative study on microbiological evaluation revealed that the aerobic colony counts for ready-to-eat food products were $10^2 - 10^8$ CFU/g for sandwiches; $10 - 10^8$ CFU/g for traditional foods; and $10^2 - 10^6$ CFU/g for dairy products and fruit juices. The highest percentage (30%) of *Listeria monocytogenes* was detected in dairy products and fruit juices and lowest in traditional foods (9.61%). The present study pointed out that attention should be dedicated to proper sanitation conditions in university canteens/street foods, and preventive measures are important for consumer protection. This study has the second major objective of assessing the food safety knowledge, attitudes, and practices of consumers and vendors employed in Islamabad's university canteens or street foods. Islamabad currently has no operational food safety legislation. Three hundred consumers and 80 vendors from four different locations (University A, University B, University C, and street food) volunteered to participate in the study. Results from the survey conducted showed that both consumers and vendors had average food safety knowledge and attitudes. Gender, age group, food safety training, education, and location did not significantly differ on the level of food safety knowledge of consumers and vendors at specific cut-off score values categorized as < 50, 50 – 75, or > 75% response level. The majority of consumers and vendors were aware of the importance of washing and cleaning hands prior to eating or food-handling with respect to foodborne diseases. Moreover, it was found during the observational study that most vendors pay attention to washing hands after money handling. However, the majority of the consumers and vendors did not know that hepatitis A, *Staphylococcus*, or *Listeriamonocytogenes* are pathogens responsible for foodborne diseases. Our results showed that proper food safety legislation should be implemented at the country level to provide biologically safe food to consumers.

Tip 84: *Introduction*

The introduction must clearly introduce each aspect of the research. If a person has zero background about the topic, the introduction gives him a clear image of the research. It's up to the writer whether he wants to add article citation in this section or not. In order to publish the article in high-impact journals, it is preferred to add citations.

Introduction:

Food is defined as an item, whether refined or raw, that is predetermined for human consumption, nourishment, and subsistence of life. One should eat healthy food. Globalization and urbanization have changed our eating habits so that one has so little time to think what they are eating is right (Ashakiran and R., 2012). It provides us with the energy and nutrients required for proper growth and nourishment, to remain healthy and active, and to perform our daily tasks energetically. Food is such an important part of our lives, it needs special attention towards its safety, including handling, preparation, and storage. Unfortunately, food safety is not that simple; despite efforts made in the forms of information campaigns and educational efforts, foodborne illness is still causing human diseases.

Awareness about food safety is at an all-time high due to new food trends occurring worldwide, and new threats are emerging to the food supply. Food safety culture is all about the people's perception of food safety, their attitude towards it, and how they behave towards food safety. It is built on the shared values of operators and their staff to provide consumers with food in the safest manner. They have to ensure that food product that is being supplied in the market is safe to consume and get feedback from the consumers to keep on checking on their services. Still, unfortunately, past studies have shown that food safety failures have gained attention across the board. According to World Health Organization (WHO), more than 200 diseases are transmitted through food. History evidenced that unsafe and unhygienic food has been a human health problem. Regardless of all efforts made by the government, foodborne illness remains a threat to human health. To overcome this issue, WHO delivered a core message of five keys to safer food that comprised: a) keep food clean b) keep separate raw and cooked food c) cook properly d) keep food at safe temperatures e) use safe water and raw materials. Recent surveys and past studies show that people are unaware of food safety, and those who know about this know the consequences, even they don't implement the food safety measures in their daily lives, and that might be the cause of the huge number of people suffering from foodborne illness today. Food safety is an alarming issue in the 21st century. It is being monitored and controlled by different agencies like the "International Association for Food Protection," "World Food Program," "World Resource Institute," "International Food and Information Council," and "Food and Agriculture Organization."

The genus *Listeria* consists of several species, out of which *Listeria monocytogenes* is considered the most pathogenic bacteria. It is a gram-positive, psychotropic, facultative anaerobic, motile, non-sporulating, small rod. It grows between 1 to 44°C, with optimum growth at 35 to 37 °C and at 7 to 10 °C, it multiplies relatively rapidly. It can grow in many foods and environments. *Listeria monocytogenes* is isolated from many environmental samples, such as soil, sewage, water, and dead vegetation. A large proportion of uncooked meat, milk, egg, seafood, and fish, as well as leafy vegetables, were found to contain this pathogen (Ray, 2004). *Listeria monocytogenes is* isolated in high frequency from different food processing and storage areas. It can grow in many foods at a refrigerated temperature, which helps it reach a low initial level to an infective dose level during storage of refrigerated foods that originally had the pathogen and those that were post-heat contaminated. The increase in consumption of many types of RTE foods stored for long periods and consumption of foods without proper reheating has increased the likelihood for the pathogen to cause the disease. Any temperature abuse, even for a short time, can accelerate the growth rate of this microorganism. *Listeria monocytogenes* is a gram-positive, rod-shaped foodborne pathogen. It is the common pathogen declared by World Health Organization (WHO) (Salazar *et al.*, 2013). It is known to cause human Listeriosis. which may lead to meningitis and cause abortion in pregnant women (Laksanalamai *et al.*, 2012). Consumption of RTE foods has been linked to the outbreak of Listeriosis; the United States reported 24 outbreaks from 1998-2008. (Cartwright *et al.*, 2013; Nelson *et al.*, 2004). CDC reported nine people from four states (California, Connecticut, Maryland, and Washington), frozen vegetables (corn, peas) were found to cause it. Recently, CDC found *a Listeria monocytogenes* outbreak, and it was linked to Dole packaged salads, and 12 people in six states were hospitalized due to infection caused by it.

Tip 85: Review of Literature

Review of literature means to have to go through past research regarding your topic. The more you review literature, the more it strengthens your document. It is necessary to provide evidence of every single word you write in this section by citation of the reference article. You can not write your opinions and views in this section. The writer may add tables and figures to understand the reader better. At the end of this section, the writer states the aims and objectives of the research. It is better to have them in bullet points.

Review of literature

Food safety and quality

Food firms' capacity to adapt manufacturing procedures that fulfill food safety and quality regulations determines their competitiveness in national and worldwide marketplaces. (Holleran and colleagues, 1999) The goal of the global food supply was to make food more affordable. Quality management systems are primarily intended to assure conformance with third-party and retailer standards. Food safety management systems are primarily responsible for controlling the specific food safety dangers connected with the product and ensuring compliance with food safety regulations (Manning and Baines, 2004).

Foodborne illness caused by *L. monocytogenes*

Listeria monocytogenes is a gram-positive, zoonotic, intracellular (Peng et al., 2016) and most common pathogen declared by World Health Organization (Salazar et al., 2013; Ueda et al., 2013). It is a causative agent of mortal foodborne illness with the capability of surviving in a wide range of environmental conditions (Jarvis et al., 2016). It is an exemplary model for studying bacterial intracellular parasitism (Cossart, 2011) rli60 (Peng et al., 2016) listeriolysin, a pore-forming toxin (Liu, 2016). Genes involved in the virulence are in LA, LC, LJ, and hlyA (Abdollahzadeh et al., 2016). Due to biofilm-forming characteristics, *L. monocytogenes* can adhere to the surfaces of equipment, persist there for a long duration, and oppose the threat to human health. It is known to infect an immune-compromised person and cause abortion in pregnant women (Chen et al., 2014; Jemmi and Stephan, 2006).

L. monocytogenes cause Listeriosis, and it deals with antibiotic treatment. It is also known to cause meningitis (brain infection), leading to a person's death. (Callejón et al., 2015). Because of unhygienic practices at the retailer level, RTE foods are known to be the major cause of Listeriosis (Chen et al., 2014). Most of the strains of *L. monocytogenes* are resistant to antibiotics, especially tetracycline. Recent research has shown that treatment of *L. monocytogenes* with other antibiotics leads to resistance against those antibiotics, which gives rise to the emergence of new strains of *L.monocytogenes* (Gandhi and Chikindas, 2007; Su et al., 2016).

Other pathogens responsible for foodborne illness

Pathogenic and nonpathogenic bacteria are differentiated from the factors causing virulence, which encode for pathogenicity and are termed "Pathogenicity Islands."(Hensel, 2004). They are acquired by lateral gene transfer (Nieto et al., 2016). Pathogenicity Islands (PALs) are a subclass of genomic islands. They are found in a wide range of both gram-positive and gram-negative bacteria (GalMor and Finlay, 2006). *Staphylococcus aureus* is a foodborne pathogen. It is found to be the main element of contamination of milk and dairy products and is known to cause disease both in livestock and humans ranging from acute skin diseases to fatal diseases like pneumonia (Guessas et al., 2007). *Staphylococcus aureus* strain, Methicillin-resistant *Staphylococcus aureus* (MRSA) CC398 is found to have a significant threat to human health. It completes its life cycle by transferring from human to livestock-linked animals then transferring back to human beings (Ballhausen et al., 2012). Past studies have shown that MRSA CC398 in humans and livestock are secretly linked. It triggers rare diseases in animals as compared to humans. In humans, it initiates diseases under specific conditions without developing any clinical symptoms (Ballhausen et al., 2012). *Staphylococcus aureus* produces extracellular proteins such as exotoxins and enzymes that enhance virulence. Genes involved in virulence are found to be *seh, sea, see, mecA , and sec*. The most frequently found gene was *sec* (Basanisi et al., 2016). In some species of *S. aureus*, virulence is enhanced by the production of biofilm, which is resistant to antimicrobial agents; thus, it makes *S.aureus* more difficult to eliminate. (Zmantar et al., 2016). The genus *salmonella* possesses two different species, i.e., *Salmonella bongori* and *Salmonella enterica,* and further classified into six subspecies (J. et al., 2012). *Salmonella enterica* is a facultative intracellular, gram-negative, rod-shaped pathogen that is associated with food poisoning, typhoid fever, and gastroenteritis. Beef, pork, poultry, milk, egg, and seafood are the most common contaminated food that causes *salmonellosis* in human (Al-Sheddy et al., 1995; Bohaychuk et al., 2006). *Salmonella serovars* are found in the intestinal tract of humans, farm animals, wild birds, reptiles, and in fewer insects (Andino and Hanning, 2015). Its pathogenicity is a foodborne pathogen that is well studied (Dickson, 1991). It is reported that Salmonella causes 95% of foodborne human infections, and it is even more injurious in developing countries (Santos et al., 2003). According to the foodborne diseases Active Surveillance Network (Food Net), millions of foodborne illness reports are registered per year due to *Salmonella* (Voetsch et al., 2004). *Salmonella enterica* serotype has a broad range of hosts within birds and mammals is the highest host adaptive pathogen and causes diseases in humans and higher primates; thus, it is a major burden to public health (Rabsch et al.,

2002). The virulence of *Salmonella serovars* is mostly encoded on the *Salmonella* Pathogenicity Islands (SPI) (J. et al., 2012). *Salmonella* virulence property is regulated by genes contained within pathogenicity islands. They are found to be SP1-1 and SP1-2. SP1-1 allows *Salmonella* to enter mammalian epithelial cells, and SP1-2 assists *Salmonella* in its survival within macrophages. Both of these islands are 40kb long and are attained by horizontal gene transfer (Hensel, 2004; Ochman and Groisman, 1996)

Table 1. Food borne pathogens and their sources and symptoms (Khan et al., 2016)

Pathogen	Source	Symptom
Listeria monocytogenes	Unpasteurized milk, soft cheese made by unpasteurized milk, ready-to-eat meats	Fever, muscle aches, nausea, diarrhea
Staphylococcus aureus	Unrefrigerated or improperly refrigerated meats potatoes and egg salads, cream pastries	Boils, lung infection, minor skin infections
Salmonella	Eggs, poultry, meat unpasteurized milk or juice cheese, contaminated raw fruits and vegetables	Abdominal cramping, gas, chills, fever, fatigue, vomiting
Escherichia coli	Water or food contaminated with human feces	Abdominal cramping, gas, loss of appetite, fever, fatigue

Food safety/nutrition awareness

To ensure food safety, "The Food Safety Modernization (FSMA) was signed as a law in the United States. Consumers, as well as food handlers, were found to lack awareness of food safety and hygiene. Appropriate training aid should be given to them to overcome foodborne disease (Samapundo *et al.*, 2015; Parry-Hanson Kunadu *et al.*, 2016). Home and Consumer (HCS) Studies are considered to be the most suitable place for food safety education. It is compulsory for all Swedish (Lange, 2016). Positive Deviance (PD) targeting people with diabetes and pregnant women was done. The objective of this program was to discuss food handling behaviors and the adoption of recommended practices (Fowles et al., 2005). A food safety and quality management system is an approach to focus on food risk management. Microbial assessment scheme determines the performance of current FSMS in the food industry. The tools are guidelines for verifying food control measures (Karaman et al., 2012).

Indicators of general microbiological quality and hygiene condition

PHLS In 2000 published the second revised guidelines for the interpretation of the results of microbiological examination of various RTE foods sampled at point of sale (Table. 2).

Table 2. Indicators of general microbiological quality and hygiene condition

Criterion	Microbiological quality (CFU/g unless stated)			
	Satisfactory	Acceptable	Unsatisfactory	Unacceptable/ Potentially hazardous
Aerobic colony count* 30°C/4 h	$<10^3$	10^3-$<10^4$	$\geq 10^4$	N/A†**
	$<10^4$	10^4-$<10^5$	$\geq 10^5$	N/A**
	$<10^5$	10^5-$<10^6$	$\geq 10^6$	N/A**
	$<10^6$	10^6-$<10^7$	$\geq 10^7$	N/A**
	N/A	N/A	N/A	N/A**
Indicator organisms††				
Enterobacteriaceae‡	<100	100-$<10^4$	$\geq 10^4$	N/A**
Escherichia coli (total)	<20	20-<100	≥ 100	N/A**
Listeria spp. (total)	<20	20-<100	≥ 100	N/A**

Pathogens				
Salmonella spp.	ND			D
Campylobacter spp.	ND			D
E. coli O157 & other VTEC	ND			D
Vibrio cholera	ND			D
Vibrio parahaemolyticus	<20	20-<100	100-<10^3	≥10^3
Listeria monocytogenes	<20	20-<100	N/A	≥100
Staphylococcus aureus	<20	20-<100	100-<10^4	≥10^4
Clostridium perfringens	<20	20-<100	100-<10^4	≥10^4
Bacillus cereus and other pathogenic Bacillus spp.	<10^3	10^3-<10^4	10^4-<10^5	≥10^5

Food packaging plays a vital role in safeguarding food all over the distribution chain; without packaging, food can be contaminated by physical, chemical, and biological contaminants (Tumwesigye et al., 2012). It can be contaminated during the processing from the reception of raw material to the final product. Contamination can come from environmental conditions in which food is stored, like preheating, disinfection, cleaning, and sterilization steps, so precautionary measures must be taken (Nerín et al., 2016). Polymer nanocomposites are being used in food packaging materials because they possess mechanical, thermal, and barrier properties (Farhoodi, 2016). However, polymers are non-biodegradable; thus, they lead to serious ecological problems and need to b replaced by eco-friendly packaging films (Duncan, 2011; Siracusa et al., 2008). Cellulose nanofibers are eco-friendly and are perceived as the most ample renewable polymeric material. Its use will lower the cost of food packaging and will reduce environmental pollution (Abdul Khalil et al., 2016). Moreover, essential oil (EO) exhibits a striking ingredient for biodegradable and eco-friendly food packaging; they add value to the product and prolong food shelf life. We can directly apply them to the food, or they can be used in food packaging material in vapors form (Krisch et al., 2011). Essential oils exhibit a striking ingredient for biodegradable and eco-friendly food packing; they add value to the product and prolong food shelf life (Abdul Khalil et al., 2016). Elevated food shelf-life grants customers high-quality food for a certain period after production. Silver nanoparticles are being used to increase food shelf life as they possess antimicrobial properties (Pulizzi, 2016; Sung et al., 2013). For example, silver montmorillonite (Ag-MMT) is capable of improving the shelf life of fruit and salad (Costa et al., 2011) to keep an eye on food packaging and processing EU legislation and compliance test novel food packaging technologies (Dainelli et al., 2008).

Overview of university and street food in Islamabad

Recent studies have shown that consumption of fresh fruits and vegetables is found to be an emerging trend, especially in those areas in which local restaurants are present and offer RTE eat foodstuff. However, the environment in which food is provided is open and unhygienic practices by the food handlers were observed, leading to numerous gastroenteritis outbreaks caused by *E. coli* (Faour et al., 2016). Due to nutritional value and antioxidant properties, consumption of vegetables and fruits is cheered by health agencies though they cause many foodborne diseases if not properly treated. A study was conducted to check the prevalence of foodborne pathogens in RTE food, and it was found that 34% of samples were contaminated with multidrug-resistant *E. coli* pathogens (Shah et al., 2015). In developing countries like Pakistan, the potential of growing antibiotic-resistant organisms is due to inadequate use of antibiotics in agricultural farms and treating the farm with untreated sewage water (Ruimy et al., 2010). A survey-based study conducted in Islamabad, Pakistan, which comprises men and women of age ranging from 20-25, showed that people and students living in hostels suffer from foodborne diseases. Knowledge about food safety and its level of awareness varied, and the food handlers observed a lack of hygiene practices. Therefore, there is a need to create awareness among the students about food safety on a serious note (Hanif *et al.*, 2015).

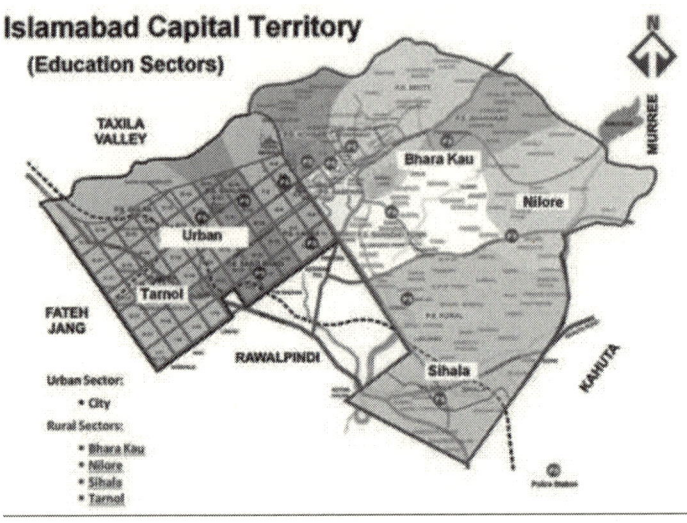

Figure 1. Map of Islamabad Capital Territory

Food safety knowledge, attitudes and handling practices in Islamabad

Foodborne diseases are of great concern all around the globe. Its incidence rate is quite high in developed countries; about 1/3 of the total population is going through it while it is at its worst stage in developing countries due to improper sanitary systems, poverty, and lack of hygiene (Fowles et al., 2005). A study was conducted to check the food quality, and it was revealed that RTE food that is available at the public level is not safe for consumption. Persistence and proliferation of epiphytic flora of fruit and vegetable depict the poor hygiene practices of the food handlers (Hannan *et al.*, 2014; Khan *et al.*, 2016) have found that in Pakistan, out of 31 pathogens, *Staphylococcus aureus* and *Listeria monocytogenes* were found to be the most common pathogens. The food industry has shown concern towards food safety and has adopted different decontamination techniques like pasteurization, ohmic heating, and high-pressure processing.

Razzaq et al. (2014) did a study regarding mixed and separate vegetables. They found a significant amount of *Staphylococcus aureus, Pseudomonas aeruginosa, E. coli, Enterobacter spp.*, and *Salmonella spp*. This depicted poor hygiene, agricultural harvesting, and the production of vegetables. He suggested that consumers should be alarmed about the situation and should adopt hygiene (Razzaq et al., 2014). Another study conducted among street vendors and food items was microbiologically examined. It was observed that Enterobacteriaceae heavily contaminated the majority of the fast food, and food is claimed to be unfit for human consumption (Khan et al., 2015).

Aims and objectives

The objective of this study includes the following:

To conduct microbiological examination (detection of *Listeria monocytogenes*) in RTE food products available from university/street foods vendors in Islamabad, Pakistan.

To evaluate the status of food safety and nutrition knowledge, attitude, and practices among vendors and consumers in Islamabad, Pakistan.

Tip 86: Materials and Methods

The researcher evaluates research conditions and limitations prior to the research proposal and designs its project accordingly, i.e., how many methods are there to do a particular experiment? Does the researcher have the required machinery, apparatus, and equipment? After analyzing these conditions, the researcher chooses the best and feasible methods for his research.

Materials and methods:

University/street food samples collection and microbial analysis

Food sampling

A total of 80 food samples were collected from four locations in Islamabad. Food samples were categorized into three main categories a) sandwiches, b) traditional food, c) dairy products, and fruit juices. Samples were collected from the canteens of the respective universities A, B, C, and street food vendors. (Table 3)

Transportation

While collecting food samples, ingredients and food processing steps were carefully registered. The samples were aseptically collected in sterile plastic pouches and sealed. The sample number, food item, and date were marked on the sterile plastic pouch. Each sterile plastic pouch carried a single sample. These sterile plastic pouches were kept in an icebox and were transported to the laboratory and treated within an hour of purchase for further processing.

Table 3. List of food items from four different locations with microbiological analysis

Food	Food product type	No of sub samples obtained	Microbiological quality indicator tested	Microbial pathogen tested
RTE	Sandwiches	18	Total aerobic counts	*Listeria monocytogenes*
	Traditional dishes	52		
	Dairy products and fruit juices	10		

Food samples processing and analysis

Preparation of peptone water (homogenization)

Peptone water was prepared by adding 1g of peptone, 0.85 NaCl, and 1ml Tween 80 in 1 liter of distilled water, and a magnetic stirrer was used for uniform homogenization. Then, peptone water was shifted to reagent bottles and autoclaved for 60 minutes at 121ºC.

Preparation of peptone water (serial dilution)

For the serial dilutions, peptone water was prepared by adding 15g of peptone in 1 liter of distilled water. The solution was then uniformly mixed using a magnetic stirrer for 20 minutes and then transferred to reagent bottles and autoclaved for 60 minutes at 121°C.

Homogenization of food

Homogenization of food was done aseptically under laminar airflow. First, a 20g of food sample was taken in a sterile plastic pouch, and 180ml of peptone was added to it. Next, homogenization was done manually for 2-3 minutes till complete homogenization. Then, food samples were treated under laminar airflow.

Serial dilution

Test tubes containing 9ml of peptone water were prepared and autoclaved a day before treating the sample. Appropriate dilutions in test tubes were obtained prior to inoculations on Petri plates.

Media preparation

Plate Count Agar

Plate Count Agar (PCA, Oxoid, UK) promotes the growth of aerobic cultures. Media was prepared by adding 12g /500ml of PCA. It was then transferred to reagent bottles and was autoclaved at 121°C, 15 psi pressure.

Palcam agar

Palcam agar (Oxoid, UK) is a selective media for *Listeria monocytogenes*. Palcam was prepared by adding 34.5g of palcam medium and 7.5g of agar in 500ml of distilled water. It was supplemented with palcam agar selective supplement (SR0150E) and poured into Petri plates.

Listeria enrichment broth

As the name shows, Listeria Enrichment Broth (LEB) was used to enrich *L. monocytogenes* in the food sample when stored at 30°C for 24 hours. For each batch, 36 grams/liter of LEB was required. It was supplemented with LEB selective supplement (SR0141E) and stored till use.

Preparation of TSB-yeast broth (for sub culturing)

The colonies of *L. monocytogenes* from food samples positive with its presence were sub-cultured in TSB-YE and incubated at 37°C along with the control (*L. monocytogenes* ATCC 13932). The cultures were then subjected to confirmatory tests.

Table 4. Conditions for the growth of Listeria monocytogenes and aerobic colony count

Microorganisms	Incubation time (h)	Temp °C	Culture Technique	Culture Media and confirmation tests
Aerobic colony count	72	30	Pour plate	Plate count Agar
Listeria monocytogenes	24	30	Enrichment	Listeria enrichment broth supplemented with SR0141E
	24	37	Streak plate	Palcam agar supplemented with SR0150E
				Green-grey colonies with black core and halo, Gram staining, catalase test, oxidase test

Bacterial identification tests

Gram staining

L. monocytogenes is a gram-positive bacterium rod-shaped. Prior to gram staining, a very little amount of culture from the test tube was transferred on a glass slide using an inoculation loop. Smear a very thin layer onto the slide using a wire loop and fix it by gently passing the slide over the flame (heat fixation). After heat fixation, four steps were performed: a) add drops of crystal violet stain on the fixed culture for 60 seconds, then pour off the stain. Rinse the excess stain with distilled water present in the bottle; b) add the drops of iodine solution on the smear, enough to cover the fixed culture for 60 seconds. Rinse the excess stain gently with distilled water; c) add drops of decolorizer on the smear. Rinse it off with distilled water after 5 seconds; d) add a few drops of Safranin (Counterstain) on the slide for 30 seconds. Then, rinse it off with distilled water. Now, air-dry the slide and then put emersion oil on smear and observe under the microscope.

Catalase test

L. monocytogenes is catalase positive. Pick one drop of the culture from the test tube (TSB-YE) using a wire loop and place the drop on the glass slide. One drop of H_2O_2 was added to it by using a dropper and then observed. The emergence of bubbles that appeared on the slide confirmed the presence of *L. monocytogenes*.

Oxidase test

L. monocytogenes is oxidase negative. For this test, filter paper strips were used. One drop of the culture from the test tube containing TSB-YE broth was picked by using a wire loop and placing the drop on filter paper strip, and added one drop of oxidase reagent using the dropper and observed it. No color change resulted in the confirmation of the presence of *L. monocytogenes*.

Food safety knowledge and attitudes questionnaire

The study was conducted in the capital of Pakistan (Islamabad). Three universities and street vendors were selected for the survey.

Eighty street vendors and 300 consumers were involved in the survey. Consumers and vendors were equally distributed between the four locations. Questionnaires were designed to determine the food safety knowledge, attitude, and practices of the consumers and vendors, and a checklist was used to evaluate the results.

Food safety knowledge and attitude questionnaire

Adoption of the questionnaire to determine vendors' and consumers' food safety knowledge and attitude was taken from (Samapundo et al., 2015). This can be observed in Tables 9-10. A pilot test was taken before starting the actual survey. A pilot test was conducted among twenty people. Slight modifications were incorporated, and we had the final version of our questionnaires. Questionnaires were categorized into four sections i) demographic, ii) food safety knowledge, iii) food safety attitude, and iv) food safety practices. Questionnaires were filled by the participants, while in the case of illiterate participants, it was filled by the researcher by asking them the questions and translating the questions for their understanding. The demographic section included the information with regard to age, gender, educational status and training regarding food safety. The food safety knowledge portion was constructed to check the information and understanding of the consumers and vendors to foodborne pathogens, personal food hygiene, proper cleaning, and high-risk groups. This section accommodated 12 questions with three possible answers--"yes," "no," and "do not know." One point was given to each right answer, while incorrect and answers responding to do not know were not given points. The score was then converted to 100 with a maximum possible score of 12 questions. A score below 50% was taken as poor knowledge of food safety. The average score was considered between 50-75%, while a score greater than 75% indicated good knowledge about food safety. A food safety attitude section was constructed to evaluate the understanding of the consumers and vendors with respect to food safety. This section also contained 12 questions with three possible answers as mentioned above. The scoring system to evaluate food safety attitude was the same as mentioned above. Selection of the consumers was made by approaching persons from 12 years and older and asking them to participate in the study voluntarily. The aim of the study was clearly explained to the participants before asking them to fill the questionnaire. The study was stopped when 75 consumers from each location completed the questionnaire and gave a total of 300 respondents. Vendors serving around targeted universities and markets nearby in each location were randomly accessed and were asked to take part willingly in the study. Like consumers, the objective of the study was made clear before handing over the questionnaire. When 20 vendors from each location completed the questionnaire, the interviews were stopped.

Food handling observation and checklist

To determine food safety practices among consumers and street vendors, a checklist was used that can be seen in (Table 22). Demographic data comprised gender, age, location, educational status, and food safety training. There were five main categories in the checklist i) environment around the stall ii) food preservation facilities at the vending site. iii) Information regarding facilities iv) cleaning and maintenance of utensils v) personal hygiene. The existence or absence of every section was recorded. The participants were selected on the same methodology as mentioned for the attitude and knowledge section. The aim of the study was made clear to the vendors and consumers, and they were asked to participate voluntarily.

Data entry and statistical analysis

The data collected from the questionnaires and the observation checklists were labeled in EPI Info 7 (CDC, US), where the scores were computed. Prior to analysis, the age and score parameters were split into different categories. For descriptive analysis of the age, cut-off points of < 20, 20 – 25, 26 – 30, and > 30 years were used. However, comparisons of scores between different age groups were limited to two groups (≤ 25 and > 25) due to the small sample size. For comparisons of scores among gender, age groups, food safety training, education, and location, cut-off points of < 50, 50 – 75, and > 75 were used.

Data was then exported to Microsoft Excel version 2007 (Microsoft, USA). Two sample *t*-tests were performed to compare 2-sample data sets such as those for gender, age group, and food safety training. The data was then exported to SPSS version 20 (IBM, USA) for further statistical analysis. Comparisons of more than two groups, such as those for education and location, were done using fixed-effect ANOVA in SPSS version 20 (IBM, USA), where LSD values were computed. Statistical differences were based on the value of $\alpha = 0.05$.

Tip 87: *Results and Discussion*

At the end of every experiment, results are recorded, and observation is made. Once all experiments are performed, results are documented and discussed. In discussion, achieved results are compared with the past studies. Results are either similar or contradictory. In this section, it is preferred to present results in tabular form to keep it simple and deducible and to avoid misconceptions.

Results and discussion:

Microbiological quality of university/street food in Islamabad

Bacterial counts in RTE foods

There was a total of 80 samples divided into three categories, i.e., i) Sandwiches, ii) Traditional food, iii) Dairy products. 18 samples were sandwiches, 52 traditional foods, and ten dairy products and fruit juices (Table 5).

Aerobic colonies were grown out of these samples. After incubation, aerobic colonies were observed on each plate, and viable colonies were counted manually. Aerobic colonies were found in the range of <10a to <108 (Table 6).

Table 5. Aerobic Colony Count in RTE food samples

Samples	n	<10[a]	10 to <10^2	10^2 to <10^3	10^3 to <10^4	10^4 to <10^5	10^5 to <10^6	10^6 to <10^7	10^7 to <10^8	Mean ± SD
Sandwiches and snacks	18	0	0	5	7	2	0	2	2	3.78 ± 1.35
Traditional food	55	3	0	14	24	8	0	2	4	3.91 ± 1.29
Dairy Products	7	0	0	3	1	2	1	0	0	3.58 ± 1.02

n: Number of samples

[a] Range in CFU/mL of product

[b] Results are expressed as the mean population size (log CFU/mL ± SD)

Incidence of food borne pathogen in RTE foods

(Table 7) shows the incidence of *L. monocytogenes* in groups of ready-to-eat foods, i.e., sandwiches, traditional food, dairy products, and fresh juices. The highest percentage of *Listeria monocytogenes* was (30%) recorded in dairy products and fresh juices, followed by sandwiches (27.7%) and traditional foods (9.61%). The incidence of potential foodborne *pathogen L.*

monocytogenes in sandwiches and traditional food is comparable to those described in previous studies (Kotzekidou, 2013)(Christison *et al.*, 2008; Little *et al.*, 2009),(Guerra *et al.*, 2001).

Table 6. Incidence of *L. monocytogenes* in RTE food products

RTE Food	*Listeria monocytogenes*
Sandwiches	5/18 (27.7%)
Traditional food	5/52 (9.61 %)
Dairy products/fruit juices	3/10 (30%)
Total	13/80 (16.25%)

Food safety knowledge, attitudes and practices of university/street food consumers and vendors in Islamabad

Demographic characteristics of university/street food consumers and vendors in Islamabad

(Table 8) shows the demographic characteristics of 380 participants, 300 consumers, and 80 vendors. In case of consumers 99 (33.0%) were females and 201 (67.0%) were males. Participants' mean age was 24.6 ± 6.7 years, ranging between 13 – 59 years. One hundred ninety-one consumers were between 20 to 25 years of age. Forty-nine were between 26 to 30 years of age. 28 consumers were < 20 while 32 where >30.

Table 7. **Demographic characteristics of university and street food consumers and vendors in Islamabad, Pakistan**

Characteristics	Consumers			Vendors		
	Number (%)	Mean	Range	Number (%)	Mean	Range

	n (%)	± stdev[a]	n (%)	± stdev[a]
Gender				
Female	99 (33.0)		3 (3.7)	
Male	201 (67.0)		77 (96.3)	
Age groups (years)		24.6 ± 6.7	13 – 59	30.9 ± 11.7	17 - 62
< 20	28 (9.3)		9 (11.2)	
20 – 25	191 (63.7)		28 (35.0)	
26 – 30	49 (16.3)		13 (16.3)	
> 30	32 (10.7)		30 (37.5)	
Education				
Illiterate	0 (0.0)		9 (11.2)	
Below high school/ < matriculation	3 (1.0)		29 (37.4)	
High school/matriculation	11 (3.7)		30 (37.5)	
Higher secondary school/intermediate	53 (17.7)		9 (11.2)	
College/university/graduate	133 (44.3)		3 (3.7)	
University/postgraduate	100 (33.3)		0 (0.0)	
Food safety training				
Yes	11 (3.7)		33 (41.2)	
No	289 (96.3)		47 (58.8)	
Location				
University A	75 (25.0)		20 (25.0)	
University B	75 (25.0)		20 (25.0)	
University C	75 (25.0)		20 (25.0)	
Street food	75 (25.0)		20 (25.0)	
Total	300		80	

[a] stdev = standard deviation.

In regard to educational status, none of the consumers was illiterate. (10%) were below matric. (37%) had education till high school. (17.7%) had higher secondary school. (44.3%) graduates and (33.3%) had a postgraduate qualification. Moreover, (96.3%) of consumers did not have any food safety training. In the case of vendors, 3 (3.7%) were female, and 77 (96.3%) were male.

Participants' mean age was 30.9 ± 1.7 years, ranging between 17 – 62 years. Nine vendors were <20, 28 were between 20-25, 13 were between 26-30, and 30 were >30. With respect to educational status (11.2%) were illiterate. (37.4%) were below matric, (37.5%) had done matric (11.2%) had done intermediate, (3.7%) were graduate and none of them had postgraduate. Regarding food safety training (41.2%) had the training, while the remaining (58.8%) of the vendors did not have any food safety training. Demographics of this study contradict with (Samapundo et al., 2015) their educational status is lower, but we lack behind in case of food safety training (70%) of their audience have food safety training, this study is in accordance with (Martins, 2006; Omemu and Aderoju, 2008; Soares et al., 2012).

Food safety knowledge of consumers and vendors

(Table 9) shows the result of food safety knowledge of consumers of universities and street food consumers in Islamabad, Pakistan. They had a mean score of 63, depicting moderate knowledge about food safety. Yet 16% of consumers have poor knowledge about food safety (score <50), while 15% of the consumers have relatively good knowledge (>75).

Table 8. Effect of gender, age, education level, food safety training, and location on the food safety knowledge of university and street food consumers in Islamabad, Pakistan

Characteristics	Number of respondents (%)			Mean score ± stdev[a]	Range
	< 50	50 – 75	> 75		
Gender					
Female	12 (4.0)	67 (22.3)	20 (6.7)	66.8 ± 16.8	33 – 100
Male	36 (12.0)	141 (47.0)	24 (8.0)	61.0 ± 15.9	25 – 92

Age groups (years)					
< 20	7 (2.3)	19 (6.3)	2 (0.7)	57.1 ± 16.4	33 – 92
20 – 25	30 (10.0)	130 (43.3)	31 (10.3)	62.7 ± 16.7	25 – 100
26 – 30	8 (2.7)	35 (11.7)	6 (2.0)	64.8 ± 14.9	33 – 92
> 30	3 (1.0)	24 (8.0)	5 (1.7)	66.4 ± 15.6	33 – 100
Education					
Illiterate	0 (0.0)	0 (0.0)	0 (0.0)	0.0 ± 0.0	0 – 0
Below high school/ < matriculation	3 (1.0)	0 (0.0)	0 (0.0)	36.0 ± 5.1	33 – 42
High school/matriculation	4 (1.3)	7 (2.3)	0 (0.0)	50.0 ± 9.8	33 – 67
Higher secondary school/intermediate	6 (2.0)	42 (14.0)	5 (1.7)	59.4 ± 14.9	25 – 92
College/university/graduate	25 (8.3)	89 (29.7)	19 (6.3)	62.1 ± 16.5	25 – 100
University/postgraduate	10 (3.3)	70 (23.3)	20 (6.7)	68.1 ± 15.7	33 – 100
Food safety training					
Yes	1 (0.3)	6 (2.0)	4 (1.3)	75.7 ± 22.8	25 – 100
No	47 (15.7)	202 (67.3)	40 (13.3)	62.5 ± 15.9	25 – 100
Location					
University A	9 (3.0)	52 (17.3)	14 (4.7)	64.4 ± 15.7	25 – 92
University B	12 (4.0)	45 (15.0)	18 (6.0)	66.3 ± 17.5	33 – 100
University C	12 (4.0)	55 (18.3)	8 (2.7)	63.4 ± 15.4	33 – 92
Street food	15 (5.0)	56 (18.7)	4 (1.3)	57.5 ± 15.8	25 – 100
Total	48 (16.0)	208 (69.3)	44 (14.7)	62.9 ± 16.1	17 – 96

[a] stdev = standard deviation

Thus this can be concluded, though consumers generally have average food safety knowledge. Still, there is a quite large number of consumers who lack adequate food safety knowledge. Findings of Food safety knowledge are similar to previous studies (Baş *et al.*, 2006; Cuprasitrut *et al.*, 2011; Samapundo et al., 2015).

Table 9. Effect of gender, age group, and FST on FSK of consumers at different response level < 50%, 50 - 75%, > 75% (mean of the scores ± SE)

Response level (%)	FSK (Consumers)								
	Gender			Age group			FST		
	Treatment	Mean ± SE[a]	P value (T-test)	Treatment	Mean ± SE[a]	P value (T-test)	Treatment	Mean ± SE[a]	P value (T-test)
< 50%	Male	37.08±0.95	0.3	≤ 25	36.33±0.93	0.01	With FST	25± 0	0.03
	Female	35.25±1.18		> 25	37.5± 1.36		Without FST	36.87 ± 0.75	
50 – 75%	Male	62.42±0.84	0.01	≤ 25	62.83± 0.79	0.8	With FST	69.33 ± 3.58	0.15
	Female	66.04±1.12		> 25	66.42± 1.06		Without FST	63.74 ± 0.66	
> 75%	Male	86.75±0.93	0.4	≤ 25	87.3±0.94	0.5	With FST	98± 2.31	
	Female	88.2±1.57		> 25	87.73±2.12		Without FST	86.35 ± 0.76	

Data presented in Table 10 shows the means of responses (%) of FSK received from consumers at different cut-off score values (< 50, 50 – 75, > 75), along with ± standard error (SE) values and also highlight the pairwise comparison of treatments means from each other at specific cut-off score values. The P-values obtained from *t*-tests (see appendix) at 0.05 levels (α) are also summarized. The P-values of gender at (response level 50-75%) were found smaller than 0.05 (α), which rejected our null hypothesis that they are not significantly different from each other. The P-values of age at (50% response level) is found smaller than 0.05 (α), which rejected our null hypothesis that they are not significantly different from each other. The P-values of age at (50-75% &>75% response level) is found greater than 0.05 (α), which accepted our null hypothesis that they are not significantly different from each other. The P-values of FST at (50% response level) are found smaller than 0.05 (α), which rejected our null hypothesis that they are not significantly different from each other. The P-values of FST at (50-75% response level) is found greater than 0.05 (α), which accepted our null hypothesis that they are not significantly different from each other.

Table 10. Effect of location and education on FSK of consumers at different response level < 50%, 50 - 75, > 75% (mean of the scores ± SE)

Response level (%)	\multicolumn{2}{c}{FSK (consumers)}			
	Location		Education		
	Treatment	Mean ± SE[a]	Treatment	Mean ± SE	
<50%	University A	34.11±1.73 a	Below matric	36±3 a	
	University B	37.5±1.36 ab	Matric	39.75±2.25 ab	
	University C	38.25±1.34 bc	Intermediate	33.33±3.11 ac	
	Street Food	36.13±1.62 abd	Graduate	37.36±1.03 bcd	
	LSD at 0.05	4.52	Postgraduate	35.7±1.37 bcde	
			LSD at 0.05	4.35	
50 – 75%	University A	64.16±1.23 a	Below matric	0±0	
	University B	65.2±1.25 ab	Matric	55.86±2.39 a	
	University C	65.38±1.27 abc	Intermediate	59.93±1.41 ab	

		Street Food	60.73±1.3 abcd	Graduate	63.81±1 abc
		LSD at 0.05	7.32	Postgraduate	35.7±.1.01 bd
				LSD at 0.05	7.24
> 75%		University A	83.69±1.62 a	Below matric	-
		University B	83.39±1.43 ab	Matric	-
		University C	87.5±1.7 abc	Intermediate	86.6±2.2 a
		Street Food	93.75±4.05 abcd	Graduate	86.68±1.37 ab
		LSD at 0.05	5.75	Postgraduate	87±1.08 ac
				LSD at 0.05	4.12

Data presented in (Table 11) shows the means of responses (%) of FSK consumers received from consumers at different cut-off score values (< 50, 50 – 75, > 75), along with ± standard error (SE) values and also highlight the comparison of treatments means from each other at specific cut-off score values. The calculated LSD value of location parameter (< 50% response level) at 0.05 levels is 4.52. University C is significantly different from university A (see appendix), showing that they are significantly different from each other. The calculated LSD value of location parameter (50-75% response level) at 0.05 levels is 7.32. The computed LSD value for all four locations is lower than the calculated LSD value (see appendix), showing that they are not significantly different. The calculated LSD value of location parameter (>75% response level) at 0.05 level is 5.75. The computed LSD value for all four locations is lower than the calculated LSD value (see appendix), showing that they are not significantly different. The calculated LSD value of the education parameter (< 50% response level) at 0.05 levels is 4.35. The computed LSD value of matric is significantly greater than the calculated LSD value of the intermediate educational level (see appendix), showing that they are not significantly different. The calculated LSD value of the education parameter (50-75% response level) at 0.05 levels is 7.24. The computed LSD value for all four education levels is lower than the calculated LSD value (see appendix), showing that they are not significantly different. The calculated LSD value of the education parameter (75% response level) at 0.05 levels is 4.12. The computed LSD value of graduates is significantly greater than the calculated LSD value of postgraduate educational level (see appendix), showing that they are significantly different from each other.

(Table 9) shows the results of food safety knowledge of universities and street food vendors in Islamabad, Pakistan. They had a mean score of 60, depicting moderate knowledge about food safety. Yet 15% of vendors have poor knowledge about food safety (score <50), while

9% of the vendors have relatively good knowledge (>75).

Table 11. Effect of gender, age, education level, food safety training, and location on the food safety knowledge of university and street food vendors in Islamabad, Pakistan

Characteristics	Number of respondents (%)			Mean score ± stdev[a]	Range
	< 50	50 – 75	> 75		
Gender					
Female	0 (0.0)	2 (2.5)	1 (1.3)	75.0 ± 8.0	67 -83
Male	12 (15.0)	59 (73.8)	6 (7.5)	59.5 ± 13.0	33 -92
Age groups (years)					
< 20	1 (1.3)	6 (7.5)	2 (2.5)	65.7 ± 13.9	42 -83
20 – 25	3 (3.8)	24 (30.0)	1 (1.3)	61.1 ± 12.5	42 -92
26 – 30	3 (3.8)	9 (11.3)	1 (1.3)	59.7 ± 13.4	42 -83
> 30	5 (6.3)	22 (27.5)	3 (3.8)	57.7 ± 13.4	33 -83
Education					
Illiterate	2 (2.5)	7 (8.8)	0 (0.0)	52.7 ± 11.1	33 -67
Below high school/ < matriculation	3 (3.8)	22 (27.5)	4 (5.0)	61.8 ± 13.4	42 -92
High school/ matriculation	5 (6.3)	23 (28.8)	2 (2.5)	60.0 ± 13.1	33 -83
Higher secondary school/intermediate	2 (2.5)	6 (7.5)	1 (1.3)	59.3 ± 14.5	42 -83
College/university/graduate	0 (0.0)	3 (3.8)	0 (0.0)	69.6 ± 4.6	67 -75
University/postgraduate	0 (0.0)	0 (0.0)	0 (0.0)	0.0 ± 0.0	0 -0
Food safety training					
Yes	2 (2.5)	28 (35.0)	3 (3.8)	64.0 ± 11.1	42 -83
No	10 (12.5)	33 (41.3)	4 (5.0)	57.4 ± 13.9	33 -92
Location					
University A	4 (5.0)	15 (18.8)	1 (1.3)	58.8 ± 13.0	42 -83
University B	1 (1.3)	15 (18.8)	4 (5.0)	65.0 ± 13.1	42 -92
University C	4 (5.0)	15 (18.8)	1 (1.3)	59.5 ± 14.0	33 -83
Street food	3 (3.8)	16 (20.0)	1 (1.3)	57.2 ± 12.0	33 -83
Total	12 (15)	61 (76)	7 (9)	60.1 ± 13.0	38 -85

[a] stdev = standard deviation

Thus, this can be concluded that though, in general, vendors have average food safety knowledge. Still, there is a quite large number of vendors which lack adequate food safety knowledge.

Table 12. Effect of gender, age group, and FST on FSK of vendors at different response level < 50%, 50 - 75%, > 75% (mean of the scores ± SE)

	FSK (vendor)								
	Gender			Age group			FST		
Response level (%)	Treatment	Mean ± SE[a]	P value (T-test)	Treatment	Mean ± SE[a]	P value (T-test)	Treatment	Mean ± SE[a]	P value (T-test)
< 50%	Male	40.5 ± 1.01		≤ 25	42.00 ± 0.00	0.32	With FST	42.00 ± 0.00	0.53
	Female			> 25	39.50 ± 1.47		Without FST	40.20 ± 1.20	
50 – 75%	Male	60.93 ± 1.06	0.11	≤ 25	62.79 ± 1.76	0.20	With FST	63.54 ± 1.59	0.06
	Female	71 ± 4		> 25	59.88 ± 1.44		Without FST	59.33 ± 1.54	
> 75%	Male	84.5 ± 1.5	0.72	≤ 25	86.00 ± 3.00	0.29	With FST	83.00 ± 0.00	0.44
	Female	83 ± 0		> 25	83.00 ± 0.00		Without FST	85.25 ± 2.25	

[a] SE = Standard error; α = 0.05

Data presented in Table 13 shows the means of responses (%) received from vendors at different cut-off score values (< 50, 50 – 75, > 75), along with ± standard error (SE) values and also highlight the pairwise comparison of treatments means from each other at specific cut-off score values. The P-values obtained from T-tests (see appendix) at 0.05 levels (α) are also summarized. The descriptive data (Table 13) shows that none of the female vendors secured FSK response less than 50%. The P-values at specific cut-off score values are found greater than 0.05 (α), which accepted our null hypothesis that they are not significantly different from each other. The obtained data indicate significant differences among gender, age group, and FST at < 50%, 50 – 75%, and > 75% response levels.

Table 13. Effect of location and education on FSK of vendors at different response level < 50%, 50 - 75%, > 75% (mean of the scores ± SE)

	FSK (vendor)			
	Location		Education	
Response level (%)	Treatment	Mean ± SE[a]	Treatment	Mean ± SE
< 50%	University A	42 ± 0 a	Illiterate	39.00 ± 3.00 a
	University B	42 ± 0 ab	Below matric	42.00 ± 0.00 b
	University C	39.75 ± 2.25 abc	Matric	40.20 ± 1.80 ac
	Street Food	39 ± 3 abcd	Intermediate	42.00 ± 0.00 bcd
	LSD at 0.05	2.25	Graduate	-
			LSD at 0.05	2.43
50 - 75%	University A	61.73 ± 2.57 a	Illiterate	59.38 ± 3.35 a
	University B	61.13 ± 1.98 ab	Below matric	60.25 ± 1.85 ab
	University C	63.27 ± 2.57 abc	Matric	62.39 ± 1.86 abc
	Street Food	59.06 ± 2.01 abcd	Intermediate	61.17 ± 4.16 abcd
	LSD at 0.05	7.33	Graduate	69.67 ± 5.47 be
			LSD at 0.05	6.51

>75%	University A	83 ± 0 a	Illiterate	-
	University B	85.25 ± 2.25 ab	Below matric	85.25 ± 2.25 a
	University C	83 ± 0 abc	Matric	83.00 ± 0.00 b
	Street Food	83 ± 0 abcd	Intermediate	83.00 ± 0.00 bc
	LSD at 0.05	1.59	Graduate	-
			LSD at 0.05	1.84

Data presented in Table 14 shows the means of responses (%) received from vendors at different cut-off score values (< 50, 50 – 75, > 75), along with ± standard error (SE) values and also highlight the comparison of treatment means from each other at specific cut-off score values. The calculated LSD value of location parameter (< 50% response level) at 0.05 levels is 2.25. The computed LSD value for all four locations is lower than the calculated LSD value (see appendix), showing that they are not significantly different. The calculated LSD value of the education parameter (< 50% response level) at 0.05 levels is 2.43. The computed LSD value of intermediate compared with illiterate is greater than calculated LSD value indicates that the FSK of vendors having intermediate level education is significantly different from illiterate vendors.

Food safety attitudes of consumers and vendors

(Table 15) shows the result of food safety attitudes of consumers of university food and street food consumers in Islamabad, Pakistan. They had a mean score of 66, depicting moderate knowledge about food safety. Yet 13% of consumers have the least food safety attitude (score <50), while 25% of the consumers have a relatively good attitude (>75).

Table 14. Effect of gender, age, education level, food safety training, and location on the food safety attitude of university and street food consumers

Characteristics	Number of respondents (%)			Mean score ± stdev[a]	Range
	< 50	50 – 75	> 75		
Gender					
Female	9 (3.0)	58 (19.3)	32 (10.7)	70.5 ± 15.5	33 – 100
Male	31 (10.3)	128 (42.7)	42 (14.0)	64.3 ± 16.9	11 – 92
Age groups (years)					
< 20	7 (2.3)	20 (6.7)	1 (0.3)	54.5 ± 13.4	33 – 83
20 – 25	27 (9.0)	116 (38.7)	48 (16.0)	66.5 ± 16.5	25 – 100
26 – 30	4 (1.3)	31 (10.3)	14 (4.7)	68.3 ± 16.5	11 – 92
> 30	2 (0.7)	19 (6.3)	11 (3.7)	72.7 ± 16.1	33 – 100
Education					
Illiterate	0 (0.0)	0 (0.0)	0 (0.0)	0.0 ± 0.0	0 – 0
Below high school/< matric	2 (0.7)	1 (0.3)	0 (0.0)	44.7 ± 21.1	25 – 67
High school/ matric	2 (0.7)	8 (2.7)	1 (0.3)	57.6 ± 14.2	33 – 83
Higher secondary school/intermediate	8 (2.7)	35 (11.7)	10 (3.3)	64.2 ± 15.6	25 – 92
College/university/graduate	21 (7.0)	79 (26.3)	33 (11.0)	65.9 ± 17.5	25 – 100
University/postgraduate	7 (2.3)	63 (21.0)	30 (10.0)	69.7 ± 15.4	11 – 92
Food safety training					
Yes	2 (0.7)	5 (1.7)	4 (1.3)	69.0 ± 24.7	25 – 100
No	38 (12.7)	181 (60.3)	70 (23.3)	66.3 ± 16.4	11 – 100
Location					
University A	9 (3.0)	46 (15.3)	20 (6.7)	68.4 ± 17.4	25 – 100

University B	9 (3.0)	42 (14.0)	24 (8.0)	68.3 ± 16.8	33 – 92
University C	12 (4.0)	48 (16.0)	15 (5.0)	63.7 ± 15.9	11 – 92
Street Food	10 (3.3)	50 (16.7)	15 (5.0)	65.0 ± 16.4	25 – 100
Total	40 (13)	186 (62)	74 (25)	66.4 ± 16.6	23.5 – 96

a stdev = standard deviation

Thus this can be concluded, though consumers generally have an average food safety attitude. Still, there is a quite large number of consumers who lack adequate food safety attitude. Findings Food safety knowledge is in accordance with previous studies (Annor and Baiden, 2011; Baş et al., 2006; Rheinländer *et al.*, 2008)

Table 15. Effect of gender, age group, and FST on FSA of consumers at different response level < 50 %, 50 - 75 %, > 75% (mean of the scores ± SE)

Response level (%)	FSA (consumers)								
	Gender			Age group			FST		
	Treatment	Mean ± SE[a]	P value (T-test)	Treatment	Mean ± SE[a]	P value (T-test)	Treatment	Mean ± SE[a]	P value (T-test)
< 50 %	Male	34.61± 1.3	0.04	≤ 25	36.68± 0.97	0.07	With FST	33.5± 8.5	0.64
	Female	40± 1.32		> 25	31± 4.78		Without FST	35.95±1.11	
50 – 75 %	Male	64.55±0.74	0.20	≤ 25	64.57±0.73	0.17	With FST	63.4±5.6	0.65
	Female	66.28±1.17		> 25	66.52± 1.21		Without FST	65.14±0.63	
> 75 %	Male	85.36±0.65	0.30	≤ 25	85.98± 0.66	0.74	With FST	93.75±4.05	-
	Female	86.84±1.02		> 25	86.38± 1.09		Without FST	85.69±0.52	

Data presented in Table 16 shows the means of responses (%) of FSK received from consumers at different cut-off score values (< 50, 50 – 75, > 75), along with ± standard error (SE) values and also highlight the pairwise comparison of treatment means from each other at specific cut-off score values. The P-values obtained from *t*-tests (see appendix) at 0.05 levels (α) are also summarized. The descriptive data (Table 16) The P-value of gender at response <50% is smaller than 0.05 (α), which rejected our null hypothesis that they are not significantly different from each other. The P-values of gender at response level (50-75% &>75%) is greater than found greater than 0.05 (α), which accepted our null hypothesis that they are not significantly different from each other. The P-values of age at (50%, 50-75% &>75% response level) are found greater than 0.05 (α), which accepted our null hypothesis that they are not significantly different from each other. The P-values of FST at (50% & 50-75% response level) are found greater than 0.05 (α), which accepted our null hypothesis that they are not significantly different from each other.

Table 16. Effect of location and education on FSA of consumers at different response level < 50%, 50 - 75%, > 75% (mean of the scores ± SE)

Response level (%)	\multicolumn{2}{c}{FSA (consumers)}			
	Location		Education		
	Treatment	Mean ± SE[a]	Treatment	Mean ± SE	
< 50%	University A	35±2.14 a	Below matric	33.5± 8.5 a	
	University B	37.5± 1.82 b	Matric	37.5± 4.5 ab	
	University C	37.25± 1.72 abc	Intermediate	36.5± 1.2 abc	
	Street Food	35.9 ± 2.23 abcd	Graduate	53.9±1.25 abcd	
	LSD at 0.05	4.20	Postgraduate	35±4.31 ace	
			LSD at 0.05	6.04	
50 – 75%	University A	66.7± 1.31 a	Below matric	67± 0 a	
	University B	65.05± 1.42 b	Matric	59.5± .98 b	
	University C	64.52± 1.09 ac	Intermediate	65.03± 1.4 ac	
	Street Food	64.27± 1.27 acd	Graduate	65.05± 0.94 d	
	LSD at 0.05	6.71	Postgraduate	65.87±1.14 acde	
			LSD at 0.05	5.99	
> 75%	University A	87.9± 1.22 a	Below matric	-	
	University B	86± 0.9 ab	Matric	83. ± 0. A	
	University C	84.2± 0.85 abc	Intermediate	83.9 ± 0.95 ab	
	Street Food	86.07± 1.7 abcd	Graduate	87±1.01 abc	
	LSD at 0.05	5.35	postgraduate	86±0.79 abcd	
			LSD at 0.05	8.80	

Data presented in Table 17 shows the means of responses (%) of FSA received from Consumers at different cut-off score values (< 50, 50 – 75, > 75), along with ± standard error (SE) values and also highlight the comparison of treatment means from each other at specific cut-off score values. The calculated LSD value of location parameter (< 50% response level) at 0.05 levels is 4.20. The computed LSD value for university A and university B locations is found to be greater than the calculated LSD value (see appendix), showing that they are significantly different. The calculated LSD value of the location parameter (50-75% response level) at 0.05 level is 6.71. The computed LSD value for university B location is found greater than the calculated LSD (see appendix), showing that they are significantly different from each other. The calculated LSD value of location parameter (> 75% response level) at 0.05 levels is 5.35. The computed LSD value for all four locations is lower than the calculated LSD value (see appendix), showing that they are not significantly different. The calculated LSD value of the education parameter (< 50% response level) at 0.05 levels is 6.04. The computed LSD value of postgraduate comparing with matric and graduate is greater than calculated LSD value indicate that the FSA of the consumer having postgraduate level education is significantly different from matric and graduate consumers. The calculated LSD value of the education parameter (50 -75% response level) at 0.05 level is 5.99. The computed LSD value of matric and graduate educational level is significantly different from calculated values of intermediate and postgraduate (see appendix), showing significance between matric, graduate and intermediate, postgraduate. The calculated LSD value of the location parameter (> 75% response level) at 0.05 levels is 8.80. The computed LSD value for all four locations is lower than the calculated LSD value (see appendix), showing that they are not significantly different.

Table 17. Effect of gender, age, education level, food safety training, and location on the food safety attitude of university and street food vendors

Characteristics	Number of respondents (%)			Mean score ± stdev[a]	Range
	< 50	50 - 75	> 75		
Gender					
Female	0 (0.0)	3 (3.8)	0 (0.0)	75.0 ± 0.0	75 - 75
Male	4 (5.0)	55 (68.8)	18 (22.5)	69.0 ± 14.7	33 - 92
Age groups (years)					
< 20	0 (0.0)	8 (10.0)	1 (1.3)	64.0 ± 15.1	50 - 92
20 – 25	1 (1.3)	22 (27.5)	5 (6.3)	67.9 ± 13.0	42 - 92
26 – 30	1 (1.3)	6 (7.5)	6 (7.5)	74.3 ± 17.6	33 - 92
> 30	2 (2.5)	22 (27.5)	6 (7.5)	69.8 ± 14.2	42 - 92
Education					
Illiterate	2 (2.5)	4 (5.0)	3 (3.8)	67.7 ± 19.6	42 - 92
Below high school/ < matric	1 (1.3)	20 (25.0)	8 (10.0)	71.9 ± 14.9	33 - 92
High school/ matric	1 (1.3)	25 (31.3)	4 (5.0)	65.3 ± 13.7	42 - 92
Higher secondary school / intermediate	0 (0.0)	6 (7.5)	3 (3.8)	75.0 ± 10.2	58 - 92
College/university/ graduate	0 (0.0)	3 (3.8)	0 (0.0)	69.6 ± 4.6	67 - 75
University/ postgraduate	0 (0.0)	0 (0.0)	0 (0.0)	0.0 ± 0.0	0 - 0
Food safety training					
Yes	1 (1.3)	25 (31.3)	7 (8.8)	72.8 ± 11.4	42 - 92
No	3 (3.8)	33 (41.3)	11 (13.8)	66.7 ± 15.9	33 - 92
Location					

University A	2 (2.5)	17 (21.3)	1 (1.3)	64.7 ± 13.2	42 - 92
University B	0 (0.0)	13 (16.3)	7 (8.8)	83.0 ± 10.0	58 - 92
University C	0 (0.0)	19 (23.8)	1 (1.3)	64.2 ± 10.5	50 - 83
Street Food	2 (2.5)	15 (18.8)	3 (3.8)	65.0 ± 14.9	33 - 92
Total	4 (5)	58 (73)	18 (23)	69.2 ± 12.2	45.8 - 89.8

[a] stdev = standard deviation

Thus, though in general vendors have an average food safety attitude, there is still a quite large number of vendors that lack adequate food safety attitude.

Table 18. Effect of gender, age group and FST on FSA of vendors at different response level < 50%, 50 - 75%, > 75% (mean of the scores ± SE)

		FSA (vendor)							
		Gender			Age group			FST	
Response level (%)	Treatment	Mean ± SE[a]	P value (T-test)	Treatment	Mean ± SE[a]	P value (T-test)	Treatment	Mean ± SE[a]	P value (T-test)
< 50%	Male	39.75±2.6	-	≤ 25	42±0	0.67	With FST	42	0.67
	Female	-		> 25	39±3		Without FST	39	
50 – 75%	Male	64.76±1.29	0.07	≤ 25	63.59±1.74	0.18	With FST	69.72	-
	Female	75±0		> 25	67±1.78		Without FST	61.94	

>75%	Male	88.5 ± 1.06		≤ 25	89±1.79	0.75	With FST	88.14	0.80
	Female	-		> 25	88.25±1.34		Without FST	88.73	

Data presented in Table 19 shows the means of responses (%) of FSK received from consumers at different cut-off score values (< 50, 50 – 75, > 75), along with ± standard error (SE) values and also highlight the pairwise comparison of treatment means from each other at specific cut-off score values. The P-values obtained from *t*-tests (see appendix) at 0.05 levels (α) are also summarized. Table 19 shows that none of the female vendors secured FSA response less than 50% and greater than 75%. The P-values of gender at response level 50-75% is greater than 0.05 (α), which accepted our null hypothesis that they are not significantly different from each other. The P-values of age at (50%, 50-75% &>75% response level) are found greater than 0.05 (α), which accepted our null hypothesis that they are not significantly different from each other. The P-values of FST at (50% &>75% response level) are found greater than 0.05 (α), which accepted our null hypothesis that they are not significantly different from each other.

Table 19. Effect of location and education on FSA of vendors at different response level < 50%, 50 - 75%, > 75% (mean of the scores ± SE)

	FSA (vendor)			
	Location		Education	
Response level (%)	Treatment	Mean ± SE[a]	Treatment	Mean ± SE
< 50%	University A	42± 1.41	Illiterate	42± 0 a

	University B	-	Below matric	33± 0 ab
	University C	-	Matric	42± 0 abc
	Street Food	37.5± 4.5	Intermediate	-
	LSD at 0.05	-	Graduate	-
	P value t-test	0.37	**LSD at 0.05**	**2.43**
50 – 75%	University A	65.82± 4.12 a	Illiterate	64.75± 5.27 a
	University B	71.43± 2.65 b	Below matric	67.16± 2.34 ba
	University C	63.21 ± 4.36 abc	Matric	62.36 ± 1.95 abc
	Street Food	67.47± 3.37 acd	Intermediate	69.5± 2.8 abcd
	LSD at 0.05	**7.33**	Graduate	69.67 ± 2.67 ade
			LSD at 0.05	**6.51**
> 75%	University A	92± 1 a	Illiterate	89±3 a
	University B	89.23± 26.31 b	Below matric	88.63± 1.65ab
	University C	83 ± 1 abc	Matric	89.75± 2.25 abc
	Street Food	86 ± 1.73 bd	Intermediate	86± 3 abcd
	LSD at 0.05	**1.59**	Graduate	-
			LSD at 0.05	**1.84**

Data presented in Table 20 shows the means of responses (%) received from vendors at different cut-off score values (< 50, 50 – 75, > 75), along with ± standard error (SE) values and also highlight the comparison of treatment means from each other at specific cut-off score values. The calculated LSD value of location parameter (50-75% response level) at 0.05 levels is 7.33. The computed LSD value for university B is greater than the calculated LSD value (see appendix), showing that they are significantly different from each other. The calculated LSD value of the location parameter (75% response level) at 0.05 levels is 1.59. The computed LSD value for university A and university B is greater than calculated LSD street food (see appendix), showing that they are significantly different from each other.

The calculated LSD value of the education parameter (< 50% response level) at 0.05 levels is 2.43. The computed LSD value for all three educational levels is lower than the calculated LSD value (see appendix), showing that they are not significantly different. The computed LSD value of intermediate (50 – 75% response level) compared with illiterate is greater than the calculated LSD value indicate that the FSK of vendors having graduate-level education is significantly different from below matric and matric of vendors.

The calculated LSD value of the education parameter (>75% response level) at 0.05 level is 1.84. The computed LSD value for all three educational levels is lower than the calculated LSD value (see appendix), showing that they are not significantly different.

Assessment of FSK/FSA of consumers and vendors

Table 21. Shows results of vendors and consumers with respect to food safety knowledge and attitude questionnaire. The table gives a better understanding of the strongest and weakest fields of food safety knowledge and attitude. The results show that 8% of consumers and 6% of vendors do not know the symptoms of foodborne illness 61% of consumers and 78% of vendors haven't heard about *Listeria and Staphylococcus*. In addition, 35% of consumers and 21% of vendors wrongly interpreted that children and older people are not at more risk of having a foodborne illness. On the positive side, 93% of consumers and 99% of vendors clearly understand that washing hands before dealing with food or wearing gloves reduces the chances of contamination. The majority of the consumers (85%) and vendors (84%) are well aware of the significance of food safe.

Table 20. Assessment of the food safety knowledge and attitude of university and street food consumers and vendors

	Consumers			Vendors		
Question	Number of responses (%)			Number of responses (%)		
	Correct	Wrong	Do not know	Correct	Wrong	Do not know
Food safety knowledge						
Vomiting, diarrhea, fever and stomach pain are symptoms of food borne illness.	261 (87.0)	15(5.0)	24(8.0)	68(85)	7(8.75)	5(6.25)
Bacteria and Virus are common agents of food borne illness.	228(76.0)	37(12.3)	35(11.7)	48(60)	11(13.75)	21(26.25)
Do you know what a bacterium is?	190 (63.3)	65(21.7)	45(15.0)	27(33.75)	14(17.5)	39(48.75)
Can *Listeria* and *Staphylococcus* cause foodborne infection?	65(21.7)	53(17.7)	182(60.7)	11(13.75)	7(8.75)	62(77.5)
Hepatitis A can transmit by the unwashed hands of infected food handler.	139(46.3)	74(24.7)	87(29.0)	55(68.75)	13(16.25)	12(15)

Hepatitis A and E are bacterial infections.	94(31.3)	106(35.3)	100(33.3)	13(16.25)	17(21.25)	50(62.5)
Children and older are at more risk of food borne disease.	244(81.3)	39(13.0)	17(5.7)	67(83.75)	10(12.5)	3(3.75)
Washing hand before work and use of gloves reduce the risk of food contamination.	278(92.7)	13(4.3)	9(3.0)	79(98.75)	1(1.25)	0(0)
The risk of food borne illness increases in fetus by the infected mother.	139(46.3)	69(23.0)	92(30.7)	54(67.5)	7(8.75)	19(2.75)
Eating and drinking at work place reduce the risk of food contamination.	184(61.3)	79(26.3)	37(12.3)	22(27.5)	45(56.25)	13(16.25)
Reheating cooked food enhance food quality.	190(63.3)	89(29.7)	21(7.0)	63(78.75)	12(15)	5(6.25)
Do you know the significance of food safety?	254(84.7)	35(11.7)	11(3.7)	67(83.75)	7(8.75)	6(7.5)

Food safety attitude

Proper food handling reduces the food borne illness.	272(90.7)	20(6.7)	8(2.7)	78(97.5)	2(2.5)	0(0)
The cooked food should not be stored for long time period.	245(81.7)	40(13.3)	15(5.0)	46(57.5)	34(42.5)	0(0)
Wearing gloves and apron are important to reduce the spreading of disease.	247(82.3)	44(14.7)	9(3.0)	73(91.25)	6(7.5)	1(1.25)
Use of contaminated water for food preparation can be	199(66.3)	74(24.7)	27(9.0)	64(80)	13(16.25)	3(3.75)

Statement						
the source of food borne disease.						
Hands without gloves, currency notes and insects can be the sources of contamination of food.	237(79.0)	35(11.7)	28(9.3)	58(72.5)	14(17.5)	8(10)
The proper adjustment of temperature for stored food can reduce the contamination of food.	217(72.3)	48(16.0)	35(11.7)	54(67.5)	20(25)	6(7.5)
The clothes of food handlers and dish towels/ paper towel can be the source of contamination.	221(73.7)	46(15.3)	33(11.0)	67(83.75)	12(15)	1(1.25)
Proper washing of meat 2 - 3 times with filtered water is important to reduce the risk of salmonellosis and listeriosis.	188(62.7)	52(17.3)	60(20.0)	54(67.5)	17(21.25)	9(11.25)
The chances of contaminations are reduced by eating properly cooked food.	242(80.7)	36(12.0)	22(7.3)	72(90)	6(7.5)	2(2.5)
Use of spoon instead of hands during food handling reduces the food contamination.	150(50.0)	127(12.0)	23(7.7)	34(42.5)	43(53.75)	3(3.75)
Refreezing the defrosted food increase its shelf life.	125(41.7)	107(35.7)	68(22.7)	58(72.5)	15(18.75)	7(8.75)
Food is free from contamination if well-cooked.	63(21.0)	201(67.0)	36(12.0)	6(7.5)	69(86.25)	5(6.25)

91% of consumers and 98% of vendors know that proper food handling reduces foodborne illness. However, 17% of consumers and 21% of vendors wrongly interpret that 2 to 3 times washing of meat is not important to reduce the risk of salmonellosis and listeriosis. Only 50% of consumers and 42% of vendors are right about using spoons instead of hands to reduce the risk of contamination. 12% of consumers and 6 % of vendors don't know whether food will be free of contamination if well-cooked or not.

Observed food safety practices of university street food in Islamabad

It was observed that the majority of the vendors (98%) wash their hands before dealing with food, 87% of them trim their nails regularly. The majority (98%) were found to wash their hands after using the toilet. 78% of the vendors use towels after a meal, while the remaining 23% don't. 74% of the vendors get supply water for drinking, while 33% get filtered water. The majority (69%) of the vendors have not noticed the temperature range for freezing food. Findings of food safety knowledge is similar to previous studies (Chukuezi, 2010; Lues *et al.*, 2006; Muinde and Kuria, 2005).

Table 21. Personal hygiene, facilities, and observed food safety practices of university and street food vendors

Observation items	Observation (%)	
	Yes (%)	No (%)
Do you wash your hands before food handling?	78 (97.5)	2 (2.5)
Do you trim your nails before dealing with the food?	70 (87.5)	10 (12.5)
Do you wash your hands after using toilet?	78 (97.5)	2 (2.5)
Do you wear apron and gloves during food handling?	34 (42.5)	46 (57.5)
Did you receive any training in food safety and hygiene?	30 (37.5)	50 (62.5)
Do you wash your hands with soap after meal?	70 (87.5)	10 (12.5)
Do you wipe your hands with towel or dish cloth after meal?	62 (77.5)	18 (22.5)
Do you properly clean the dirty/used utensils with detergents and soap?	69 (86.3)	11 (13.8)
Do you regularly clean your kitchen?	76 (95.0)	4 (5.0)
Do you get water for drinking and cooking from supply water?	59 (73.8)	21 (26.3)
Do you get water for drinking and cooking from filtered water?	26 (32.5)	54 (67.5)
Do you notice the temperature range for freezing food? If yes, please specify range_____.	25 (3.3)	55 (68.8)

Tip 88: *Conclusion*

In this section, the researcher concludes their research by stating the main points in a nutshell.

Conclusion:

The study aimed to determine the microbial evaluation of food provided to a mass population from universities and street food and to determine food safety knowledge, attitude, and practices among the consumers and vendors in Islamabad, Pakistan. This study was the first of its kind that has ever been done in universities in Islamabad. Food safety is not that simple despite efforts made in the form of information campaigns and educational efforts. Foodborne illness is still causing human diseases. *Listeria monocytogenes*, in particular, is a common foodborne pathogen responsible for causing foodborne illness, and recently in 2016, its outbreak has been reported. Despite the awareness, food safety is being neglected, due to which we are unable to overcome foodborne diseases. Some observed findings of great interest were vendors and consumers did not know about the foodborne pathogens. They were unaware of groups at risk of foodborne illness. In the observational section of the study, it was found that the majority of the vendors wash their hands before dealing with the food. The majority of the vendors don't know the accurate temperature to freeze the food. Few of the vendors had food safety training. Therefore, there is a need to organize the formal training of the vendors so that they provide hygienic and safe food to consume. Though there is food safety legislation in Pakistan, there is still a need to work on food safety aspects. The findings of this study can provide momentum for legislation to be developed even better and serve Pakistan with safe and healthy food.

Tip 89: Bibliography

This section includes all the article references that were incorporated in the research. In addition, the citation includes the author's name, co-author's name, the article's title, journal name ISSN of the journal, and published year.

Bibliography:

Abdollahzadeh E, Ojagh SM, Hosseini H, Irajian G and Ghaemi EA. Prevalence and molecular characterization of *Listeria* spp. and *Listeria monocytogenes* isolated from fish, shrimp, and cooked ready-to-eat (RTE) aquatic products in Iran. LWT - Food Science and Technology, 73:205-211 (2016).

Abdul Khalil HPS, Davoudpour Y, Saurabh CK, Hossain MS, Adnan AS, Dungani R, Paridah MT, Islam Sarker MZ, Fazita MRN, Syakir MI and Haafiz MKM. A review on nanocellulosic fibers as new material for sustainable packaging: Process and applications. Renewable and Sustainable Energy Reviews, 64:823-836 (2016).

Al-Sheddy I, Fung, C. DY and Kastner CL. Microbiology of fresh and restructured lamb meat: a review. Critical reviews in microbiology, 21:31-52 (1995).

Andino A and Hanning I. Salmonella enterica: survival, colonization, and virulence differences among serovars. Salmonella enterica: survival, colonization, and virulence differences among serovars, 2015:(2015).

Annor GA and Baiden EA. Evaluation of food hygiene knowledge attitudes and practices of food handlers in food businesses in

Accra, Ghana. Evaluation of food hygiene knowledge attitudes and practices of food handlers in food businesses in Accra, Ghana, 2:830 (2011).

Ashakiran and R. D. Fast Foods and their Impact on Health. Journal of Krishna Institute of Medical Sciences University, 1:(2012).

Ballhausen B, Kriegeskorte A, van Alen S, Jung P, Köck R, Peters G, Bischoff M and Becker K. The pathogenicity and host adaptation of livestock-associated MRSA CC398. Veterinary Microbiology, (2012).

Baş M, Ersun AŞ and Kıvanç G. The evaluation of food hygiene knowledge, attitudes, and practices of food handlers' in food businesses in Turkey. The evaluation of food hygiene knowledge, attitudes, and practices of food handlers' in food businesses in Turkey, 17:317-322 (2006).

Basanisi M, Nobili G, La Bella G, Russo R, Spano G, Normanno G and La Salandra G. Molecular characterization of Staphylococcus aureus isolated from sheep and goat cheeses in southern Italy. Small Ruminant Research, 135:17-19 (2016).

Bohaychuk, Gensler, King RK, Manninen, Sorensen O, Wu J, Stiles M and McMullen L. Occurrence of pathogens in raw and ready-to-eat meat and poultry products collected from the retail marketplace in Edmonton, Alberta, Canada. Journal of Food Protection®, 69:2176-2182 (2006).

Callejón R, Rodríguez-N., Ubeda C, Ortega R, Parrilla MC and Troncoso AM. Reported foodborne outbreaks due to fresh produce in the United States and European Union: trends and causes. Foodborne pathogens and disease, 12:32-38 (2015).

Cartwright E, Jackson, A. K, Johnson, D. S, Graves LM, Silk BJ and Mahon BE. Listeriosis outbreaks and associated food vehicles, United States, 1998–2008. Emerg Infect Dis, 19:1-9 (2013).

Chen M, Wu Q, Zhang J and Wang J. Prevalence and characterization of Listeria monocytogenes isolated from retail-level ready-to-eat foods in South China. Food Control, 38:1-7 (2014).

Christison C, Lindsay D and Von Holy A. Microbiological survey of ready-to-eat foods and associated preparation surfaces in retail delicatessens, Johannesburg, South Africa. Microbiological survey of ready-to-eat foods and associated preparation surfaces in retail delicatessens, Johannesburg, South Africa, 19:727-733 (2008).

Chukuezi CO. Food safety and hyienic practices of street food vendors in Owerri, Nigeria. Food safety and hyienic practices of street food vendors in Owerri, Nigeria, 1:50 (2010).

Cossart P. Illuminating the landscape of host–pathogen interactions with the bacterium *Listeria monocytogenes*. Proceedings of the National Academy of Sciences, 108:19484-19491 (2011).

Costa C, Conte A, Buonocore GG and Del Nobile MA. Antimicrobial silver-montmorillonite nanoparticles to prolong the shelf life of fresh fruit salad. International Journal of Food Microbiology, 148:164-167 (2011).

Cuprasitrut T, Srisorrachatr S and Malai D. Food safety knowledge, attitude and practice of food handlers and microbiological and chemical food quality assessment of food for making merit for monks in Ratchathewi district, Bangkok. Food safety knowledge, attitude and practice of food handlers and microbiological and chemical food quality assessment of food for making merit for monks in Ratchathewi district, Bangkok, 2:27-34 (2011).

Dainelli D, Gontard N, Spyropoulos D, Beuken E and Tobback P. Active and intelligent food packaging: legal aspects and safety concerns. Trends in Food Science & Technology, 19, Supplement 1:S103-S112 (2008).

Dickson JS. Attachment ofSalmonella typhimurium andListeria monocytogenes to beef tissue: effects of inoculum level, growth temperature and bacterial culture age. Food Microbiology, 8:143-151 (1991).

Duncan TV. Applications of nanotechnology in food packaging and food safety: Barrier materials, antimicrobials and sensors. Journal of Colloid and Interface Science, 363:1-24 (2011).

Faour D, Todd E and Kuri V. Microbiological quality of ready-to-eat fresh vegetables and their link to food safety environment and handling practices in restaurants. LWT-Food Science and Technology, 74:224-233 (2016).

Farhoodi M. Nanocomposite Materials for Food Packaging Applications: Characterization and Safety Evaluation. Food Engineering Reviews, 8:35-51 (2016).

Fowles E, Hendricks J and Walker LO. Identifying healthy eating strategies in low-income pregnant women: applying a positive deviance model. Health care for women international, 26:807-820 (2005).

GalMor O and Finlay BB. Pathogenicity islands: a molecular toolbox for bacterial virulence. Cellular microbiology, 8:1707-1719 (2006).

Gandhi M and Chikindas ML. Listeria: a foodborne pathogen that knows how to survive. International journal of food microbiology, 113:1-15 (2007).

Guerra M, McLauchlin J and Bernardo F. Listeria in ready-to-eat and unprocessed foods produced in Portugal. Listeria in ready-to-eat and unprocessed foods produced in Portugal, 18:423-429 (2001).

Guessas B, Hadadji M, Saidi N and Kihal M. Inhibition of Staphylococcus aureus growth by lactic acid bacteria in milk. African Crop Science Conference Proceedings, 8:1159-1163 (2007).

Hanif A, Ashar SM, Rehman MU, Shaheen N and Yasmeen S. Symptoms Based Assessment of Food Borne Diseases among the Hostelide Students Living in Islamabad, Pakistan. Symptoms Based Assessment of Food Borne Diseases among the Hostelide Students Living in Islamabad, Pakistan, 5:(2015).

Hannan A, Rehman R, Saleem S, Khan M, Qamar M and Azhar H. Microbiological analysis of ready-to-eat salads available at different outlets in Lahore, Pakistan. International Food Research Journal, 21:(2014).

Hensel M. Evolution of pathogenicity islands of Salmonella enterica. International Journal of Medical Microbiology, 294:95-102 (2004).

Holleran E, Bredahl M and Zaibet L. Private incentives for adopting food safety and quality assurance. Food Policy, 24:669-683 (1999).

J. d, K. H, Parry CM, van der Poll T and Wiersinga W. Host–pathogen interaction in invasive salmonellosis. PLOS pathog, 8:e1002933 (2012).

Jarvis NA, O'Bryan CA, Ricke SC, Johnson MG and Crandall PG. A review of minimal and defined media for growth of Listeria monocytogenes. Food Control, 66:256-269 (2016).

Jemmi T and Stephan R. *Listeria monocytogenes*: food-borne pathogen and hygiene indicator. *Listeria monocytogenes*: food-borne pathogen and hygiene indicator, 25:571-580 (2006).

Karaman AD, Cobanoglu F, Tunalioglu R and Ova G. Barriers and benefits of the implementation of food safety management systems among the Turkish dairy industry: A case study. Food Control, 25:732-739 (2012).

Khan I, Miskeen S, Khalil A, Phull A, Kim S and Oh D. Foodborne Pathogens: Staphylococcus aureus and Listeria monocytogenes An Unsolved Problem of the Food Industry. Pakistan Journal of Nutrition, 15:505 (2016).

Khan I, Shah M, Mehmood F, Saeed A and Sualeh M. Determination and Identification of Enterobacteriaceae in Street Vended

Foods in Karachi, Pakistan. Pakistan Journal of Nutrition ,14:225 (2015).

Kotzekidou P. Microbiological examination of ready-to-eat foods and ready-to-bake frozen pastries from university canteens. Microbiological examination of ready-to-eat foods and ready-to-bake frozen pastries from university canteens, 34:337-343 (2013).

Krisch J, Tserennadmid R and Vágvölgyi C. Essential oils against yeasts and moulds causing food spoilage. Science against microbial pathogens: Communicating current research and technological advances, Badajoz, Spain, (2011).

Laksanalamai P, Joseph LA, Silk BJ, Burall LS, Tarr C, Gerner-Smidt P and Datta A. Genomic characterization of Listeria monocytogenes strains involved in a multistate listeriosis outbreak associated with cantaloupe in US. PLoS One, 7:e42448 (2012).

Lange M. Self-Reported Food Safety Perception Among Home and Consumer Studies Students in Relation to Knowledge and Trust. IAFP's 12th European Symposium on Food Safety, (2016).

Little C, Sagoo S, Gillespie I, Grant K and McLauchlin J. Prevalence and level of Listeria monocytogenes and other Listeria species in selected retail ready-to-eat foods in the United Kingdom. Prevalence and level of Listeria monocytogenes and other Listeria species in selected retail ready-to-eat foods in the United Kingdom, 72:1869-1877 (2009).

Liu D. Molecular detection of human viral pathogens. Molecular detection of human viral pathogens, (2016).

Lues JF, Rasephei MR, Venter P and Theron MM. Assessing food safety and associated food handling practices in street food vending. Assessing food safety and associated food handling practices in street food vending, 16:319-328 (2006).

Manning L and Baines. Effective management of food safety and quality. British Food Journal, 106:598-606 (2004).

Martins J. Socio-economic and hygiene features of street food vending in Gauteng. Socio-economic and hygiene features of street food vending in Gauteng, 19:18-25 (2006).

Muinde O and Kuria E. Hygienic and sanitary practices of vendors of street foods in Nairobi, Kenya. Hygienic and sanitary practices of vendors of street foods in Nairobi, Kenya, 5:(2005).

Nelson KE, Fouts DE, Mongodin EF, Ravel J, DeBoy RT, Kolonay JF, Rasko DA, Angiuoli SV, Gill SR and Paulsen IT. Whole genome comparisons of serotype 4b and 1/2a strains of the food-borne pathogen Listeria monocytogenes reveal new insights into the core genome components of this species. Whole genome comparisons of serotype 4b and 1/2a strains of the food-borne pathogen Listeria monocytogenes reveal new insights into the core genome components of this species, 32:2386-2395 (2004).

Nerín C, Aznar M and Carrizo D. Food contamination during food process. Trends in Food Science & Technology, 48:63-68 (2016).

Nieto PA, Pardo-Roa C, Salazar-Echegarai FJ, Tobar HE, Coronado-Arrázola I, Riedel CA, Kalergis AM and Bueno SM. New insights about excisable pathogenicity islands in Salmonella and their contribution to virulence. Microbes and Infection 18:302-309 (2016).

Ochman H and Groisman EA. Distribution of pathogenicity islands in Salmonella spp. Infection and immunity, 64:5410-5412 (1996).

Omemu A and Aderoju S. Food safety knowledge and practices of street food vendors in the city of Abeokuta, Nigeria. Food safety knowledge and practices of street food vendors in the city of Abeokuta, Nigeria, 19:396-402 (2008).

Parry-Hanson Kunadu A, Ofosu DB, Aboagye E and Tano-Debrah K. Food safety knowledge, attitudes and self-reported practices of food handlers in institutional foodservice in Accra, Ghana. Food safety knowledge, attitudes and self-reported practices of food handlers in institutional foodservice in Accra, Ghana, 69:324-330 (2016).

Peng Y, Meng Q, Qiao J, Xie K, Chen C, Liu T, Hu Z, Ma Y, Cai X and Chen C. The roles of noncoding RNA Rli60 in regulating the virulence of Listeria monocytogenes. Journal of Microbiology, Immunology and Infection, 49:502-508 (2016).

Pulizzi F. Nanotechnology in food: Silver-lined packaging. Nature Nanotechnology, (2016).

Rabsch W, Andrews HL, Kingsley RA, Prager R, Tschäpe H, Adams LG, Bäumler and J. A. Salmonella enterica serotype

Typhimurium and its host-adapted variants. Infection and Immunity, 70:2249-2255 (2002).

Razzaq R, Farzana K, Mahmood S and Murtaza G. Microbiological Analysis of Street Vended Vegetables in Multan City, Pakistan: A Public Health Concern. Pakistan J. Zool, 46:1133-1138 (2014).

Rheinländer T, Olsen M, Bakang JA, Takyi H, Konradsen F and Samuelsen H. Keeping up appearances: Perceptions of street food safety in urban Kumasi, Ghana. Keeping up appearances: Perceptions of street food safety in urban Kumasi, Ghana, 85:952-964 (2008).

Ruimy R, Cherif D, Momcilovic S, Arlet G, Andremont A and Courvalin P. RAHN-2, a chromosomal extended-spectrum class A β-lactamase from Rahnella aquatilis. Journal of antimicrobial chemotherapy, dkq178 (2010).

Salazar JK, Wu Z, McMullen PD, Luo Q, Freitag NE, Tortorello ML, Hu S and Zhang W. PrfA-like transcription factor gene lmo0753 contributes to L-rhamnose utilization in Listeria monocytogenes strains associated with human food-borne infections. Applied and environmental microbiology, 79:5584-5592 (2013).

Samapundo S, Climat R, Xhaferi R and Devlieghere F. Food safety knowledge, attitudes and practices of street food vendors and consumers in Port-au-Prince, Haiti. Food safety knowledge, attitudes and practices of street food vendors and consumers in Port-au-Prince, Haiti, 50:457-466 (2015).

Santos RL, Tsolis RM, Bäumler AJ and Adams LG. Pathogenesis of Salmonella-induced enteritis. Brazilian Journal of Medical and Biological Research, 36:03-12 (2003).

Shah M, Eppinger M, Ahmed S, Shah A, Hameed A and Hasan F. Multidrug-resistant diarrheagenic E. coli pathotypes are associated with ready-to-eat salad and vegetables in Pakistan. Journal of the Korean Society for Applied Biological Chemistry, 58:267-273 (2015).

Siracusa V, Rocculi P, Romani S and Dalla Rosa M. Biodegradable polymers for food packaging: a review. Trends in Food Science & Technology, 19:634-643 (2008).

Soares LS, Almeida RC, Cerqueira ES, Carvalho JS and Nunes IL. Knowledge, attitudes and practices in food safety and the presence of coagulase-positive staphylococci on hands of food handlers in the schools of Camaçari, Brazil. Knowledge, attitudes and practices in food safety and the presence of coagulase-positive staphylococci on hands of food handlers in the schools of Camaçari, Brazil, 27:206-213 (2012).

Su X, Zhang, Shi W, Yang X, Li Y, Pan H, Kuang D, Xu X, Shi X and Meng J. Molecular characterization and antimicrobial susceptibility of Listeria monocytogenes isolated from foods and humans. Food Control, 70:96-102 (2016).

Sung S, Sin L, Tee T, Bee S-T, Rahmat A, Rahman W, Tan A-C and Vikhraman M. Antimicrobial agents for food packaging applications. Trends in Food Science & Technology, 33:110-123 (2013).

Tumwesigye K, Oliveira J and Sousa-Gallagher M. Food Packaging and Shelf Life. Food Engineering Reviews, (2012).

Ueda S, Iwase M and Kuwabara Y. Evaluation of immunochromatography for the rapid and specific identification of Listeria monocytogenes from food. Biocontrol science, 18:157-161 (2013).

Voetsch AC, G. V, J. T, J. F, M. M, Sue., Ruthanne, Cieslak, Deneen and V. R. FoodNet estimate of the burden of illness caused by nontyphoidal Salmonella infections in the United States. Clinical Infectious Diseases, 38:S127-S134 (2004).

Zmantar T, Miladi H, Kouidhi B, Chaabouni Y, Slama R, Bakhrouf A, Mahdouani K and Chaieb K. Use of juglone as antibacterial and potential efflux pump inhibitors in *Staphylococcus aureus* isolated from the oral cavity. Microbial Pathogenesis, 101:44-49 (2016).

Tip 90: Chapter No 4 Summary

- Abstract is a kind of summary of the whole article. It includes major points from the introduction, methodology results, and discussion. It is ideal to have a one-page abstract.
- Introduction must introduce each aspect of the research clearly in such a manner that if a person has zero background about the topic, the introduction gives him a clear image of research. It's up to the writer whether he wants to add article citation in this section. In order to publish the article in high-impact journals, it is preferred to add citations.
- Review of literature means to have to go through past research regarding your topic; the more you do a review of literature, the more it strengthens your document. It is necessary to provide evidence of every word you write in this

section by citation of the reference article. You cannot write your opinions and views in this section. The writer may add tables and figures for a better understanding of the reader. At the end of this section, the writer states the aims and objectives of the research. It is better to have them in bullet points.
- In Results and Discussion, At the end of every experiment, results are recorded, and observation is made. Once all experiments are performed, results are documented and discussed. In discussion, achieved results are compared with the past studies. Results are either similar or contradictory. In this section, it is preferred to present results in tabular form to keep it simple and deducible and to avoid misconceptions.
- In conclusion, the researcher concludes their research by stating the main points in a nutshell.
- Bibliography includes all the article references that were incorporated in the research. Citation includes the author name, co-author name, the title of the article, journal name ISSN no of the journal, and year of the article publication.

Chapter 5: Scope and Future Perspectives of Microbiology

Tip 91: Scope of Microbiology

Microbiologists are in high demand in a wide range of companies and sectors nowadays. Without limiting myself to just one, here are some of the most in-demand fields and places where microbiology's breadth is clearly visible:

- Environmental Science
- Genetic Engineering
- Pollution control boards
- Hospitals
- Research Centers
- Food Microbiology
- Healthcare and Medicine
- Agrochemistry biotechnology
- Biorefineries
- Universities
- Forensic Labs

Tip 92: Food Microbiology

Microorganisms are employed in the food industry to make pickles, cheese, vinegar, wine, bread, green olives, and a variety of other foods.

Tip 93: Environmental Microbiology

The field of microbiology has a wide range of applications in this industry. Microbiologists can work on a wide range of topics in this subject, from understanding and employing bacteria (primary decomposers) to bioremediation and pest management.

Tip 94: Healthcare Sector

Bacteria and other microorganisms are utilized to produce different antibiotics and synthesize vitamins required by the body. They are also employed in gene therapy, which is used to cure genetic illnesses. As a result, the breadth of microbiology in this sector is expanding.

Tip 95: Genetic Engineering

Because of the growing popularity of the topic, the breadth of microbiology in this domain is enormous. For example, microbes' genes are modified to generate useful and valuable products such as hormones, enzymes, and so on.

Tip 96: Careers in Microbiology

With growing awareness of the importance of Microbiology, many individuals are flocking to this subject to pursue some of the high-paying courses available after 12th grade. The following are the top Microbiology jobs:

- Biotechnologist
- Medicinal Chemist
- Immunologist
- Microbiologist
- Professor
- Food technologist/Scientist
- Clinical Research Associate
- Research assistant
- Quality assurance technologists
- Food Microbiologist
- Pharmacologist
- Mycologist
- Biomedical scientist
- Water quality laboratory technician

- Cosmetic Scientists
- Sales or technical representative
- Clinical and veterinary Microbiologist

Biotechnologist

A biotechnologist conducts significant studies on the physical, chemical, and genetic features of microorganisms to conceive and build products that may be utilized in various applications. The scope of microbiology as a biotechnologist is extensive, ranging from agriculture and pharmaceutics to genetics and food sciences.

Medicinal Chemist

Medicinal chemists play an important role in the pharmaceutical industry by identifying, designing, and optimizing medications utilizing chemical molecules. As a medicinal chemist, the scope of microbiology includes not only inventing novel drug compositions but also devising new processes for drug production. This is an excellent opportunity for people who wish to pursue a career in biochemistry.

Food Microbiologist

When it comes to the breadth of microbiology, food microbiologist is a frequent job title. These specialists seek to avoid foodborne infections by performing significant studies on disease-causing bacteria, their environments, food packing, food poisoning, laws, and so on. Under this profile, you can work at educational institutes, non-governmental organizations, government and private agencies, and so on, and you can broaden your expertise by pursuing a career in food biotechnology or similar subjects.

Pharmacologist

As previously said, the scope of microbiology is not limited to certain disciplines but also has applications in other industries. One profession in which microbiologists are in high demand is that of a pharmacologist. The primary responsibility of such individuals is to identify and analyze the relationship between biological components and chemicals in order to develop new pharmaceutical goods.

Nanotechnologist

Nanotechnology courses cover chemistry, biology, physics, pharmacology, microbiology, and other subjects that have applications in practically every industry. From recognizing and treating infectious illnesses to water and sewage treatment, the scope of Microbiology as a Nanotechnologist is vast.

Technical Brewer

Technical brewers are senior-level experts in the beer manufacturing business that monitor, manage, and maintain the brewing process and equipment using their management and technical skills. Such professionals should be well-versed in biochemistry, microbiology, and so on.

Clinical Scientist

Clinical scientists work in hospitals, clinics, labs, and research institutions to use their expertise in medicine and biomedical research to aid in the growth of living creatures and produce various drugs and therapies for it.

Biomedical Scientist

A biomedical scientist often works in laboratories with healthcare professionals such as doctors or pharmacists to diagnose and manage various diseases using a collection of fluids, biopsies, and other materials.

Forensics Scientist

Microbiology's reach may also be seen in forensic sciences. These specialists evaluate evidence from crime scenes and write legal statements for court proceedings using analytical and scientific expertise and skills. They are mostly involved in laboratory analysis or crime scene investigations.

Tip 97: Microbiology Courses

Now that you're aware of the basic career profiles and prospects available in the large area of Microbiology, here are the major undergraduate, postgraduate, and Ph.D. programs you may pursue.

Bachelor's level

- BSc Hons Biology (Microbiology)
- BSc in Applied Microbiology
- BSc in Food Microbiology
- BSc in Cell & Molecular Biology
- BSc Microbiology
- BSc in Industrial Microbiology
- BSc in Clinical Microbiology

Master's level

- Master of Applied Science (Microbiology)
- MSc in Clinical Microbiology
- Master's in Molecular Biology & Biotechnology
- MSc in Microbial Genetics and Bioinformatics

- Master's in Drug Delivery and Microbiology (Research)
- <u>MSc in Medical Microbiology</u>
- Master's in Microbiology

Doctoral level

- <u>Ph.D. in Microbiology</u>
- Ph.D. in Drug Delivery and Microbiology (Research)
- DMed in Medical Microbiology
- Ph.D. in Microbiology & Immunology

Tip 98: Popular Specializations

- Agricultural Microbiology
- Evolutionary Microbiology
- Cellular Microbiology
- Veterinary Microbiology
- Microbial
- Pharmaceutical Microbiology
- Environmental Microbiology
- Industrial Microbiology
- Nano Microbiology
- Soil Microbiology
- Generation Microbiology
- Water Microbiology
- Microbial Genetics

Tip 99: Eligibility criteria

The following are the primary qualifying requirements for a profession in Microbiology:

- For Microbiology courses beyond the 12th, the applicant must have finished 10+2 with science subjects, preferably BiPC.
- For master's level microbiology studies, you must have a degree in Biology, Microbiology, or a similar specialization.

In addition, colleges in India may also require NEET PG/AIIMS PG/JIPMER results, among others things.
- If you wish to study Microbiology in another country, you may need to submit ACT/SAT results for bachelor's level courses and GRE scores for master's level courses. In addition, you must also give English proficiency scores such as IELTS/TOEFL and an SOP and LORs.

Tip 100: Top Universities for Microbiology Programs

The following universities around the globe are well-known for their world-class educational infrastructure, in addition to providing a healthy study atmosphere and quality instruction. Furthermore, the breadth of microbiology expands due to their well-structured courses and industry exposure supplied for a greater knowledge of the ideas.

- Harvard University
- University of Tokyo
- Yale University
- The University of Queensland
- University of Hong Kong
- University of Oxford
- University of Copenhagen
- Imperial College London
- University of California -Berkeley
- University of Cambridge
- Massachusetts Institute of Technology
- McGill University
- Erasmus University Rotterdam
- Seoul National University

FAQs

What is the scope and significance of microbiology?

Microbiology is an applied discipline having broad consequences in genetics, biochemistry, food science, ecology, immunology, agriculture, medicine, and many other domains. They are the most valuable biotechnological resource, despite their small size.

What are the eight branches of microbiology?

The following are the eight branches of microbiology:

Bacteriology: Bacteriology is the scientific study of bacteria.

Immunology: Immunology is the scientific study of the immune system. It investigates the interactions between pathogens like bacteria and viruses and their hosts.

Mycology: Mycology is the study of fungi like yeasts and molds. The study of nematodes is known as nematology (roundworms).

Parasitology: The study of parasites is known as parasitology. Although not all parasites are microbes, many are. Protozoa and bacteria may both be parasitic; the study of bacterial parasites is typically classified as a subfield of bacteriology.

Phycology: The study of algae is known as phycology.

Protozoology: Protozoology is the study of protozoa, which are single-celled creatures such as amoebae.

Virology: The study of viruses is known as virology.

Is microbiology a viable career path?

Microbiology is a booming subject with several career opportunities for qualified persons. The bulk of applied research programs in which microbiologists are involved require experts from a number of disciplines, including geology, chemistry, and medicine.

Is there a need for microbiologists?

Microbiologists' employment is predicted to grow at a 5% annual rate between 2020 and 2030, which is slower than the national average for all occupations. However, despite moderate employment growth, over the next decade, around 2,000 new opportunities for microbiologists are predicted to be created each year on average.

Is a microbiologist a physician?

A doctor with a medical degree specializes in microbiology and treats patients with infections. Microbiologists, both physicians, and non-physicians operate in this laboratory to help supervise and assess the work.

As a result, the reach of microbiology can be seen in practically every major area. Needless to say, with so many institutions to choose from, deciding on the best educational institute and degree combination can be a difficult endeavor. Use Leverage Edu's AI tool to get a list of the best appropriate colleges depending on your career aspirations.

About the Expert

This book is written by Sehrish Siddique a postgraduate student of COMSATS University Islamabad, Pakistan. In biology, "Bacteria" were her all-time favorites. Her interest in bacteria led her to choose Bachelors in Biosciences. She did food testing of over 80 food samples and a survey study of food safety KAP (Knowledge, attitude and practices) study of 600 sample size. This project made microbiology her passion. She did a Master's from the same university in Microbiology and Immunology. She did detailed research on antibiotic sensitivity testing and suggested Vanillin and Carbohydrate as the best alternative through experimentations and research considering antibiotic resistance to all present antibiotics. She has planned to bring these antibiotics alternative in a clinical trial after converting them to eatable form. We are looking forward to this revolution.'

HowExpert publishes how to guides by everyday experts. Visit HowExpert.com to learn more.

Recommended Resources

- HowExpert.com – Quick 'How To' Guides on All Topics from A to Z by Everyday Experts.
- HowExpert.com/free – Free HowExpert Email Newsletter.
- HowExpert.com/books – HowExpert Books
- HowExpert.com/courses – HowExpert Courses
- HowExpert.com/clothing – HowExpert Clothing
- HowExpert.com/membership – HowExpert Membership Site
- HowExpert.com/affiliates – HowExpert Affiliate Program
- HowExpert.com/jobs – HowExpert Jobs
- HowExpert.com/writers – Write About Your #1 Passion/Knowledge/Expertise & Become a HowExpert Author.
- HowExpert.com/resources – Additional HowExpert Recommended Resources
- YouTube.com/HowExpert – Subscribe to HowExpert YouTube.
- Instagram.com/HowExpert – Follow HowExpert on Instagram.
- Facebook.com/HowExpert – Follow HowExpert on Facebook.
- TikTok.com/@HowExpert – Follow HowExpert on TikTok.

Made in the USA
Columbia, SC
14 January 2024

89788a8f-e7c9-4440-abc8-2c65311a4df4R05